THE COMPLETE BOOK OF

Laser Sailing

Dick Tillman

WITH A FOREWORD BY

Bruce Kirby

INTERNATIONAL MARINE / McGRAW-HILL

Camden, Maine ▪ New York ▪ San Francisco ▪ Washington, D.C. ▪ Auckland
Bogotá ▪ Caracas ▪ Lisbon ▪ London ▪ Madrid ▪ Mexico City ▪ Milan ▪ Montreal
New Delhi ▪ San Juan ▪ Singapore ▪ Sydney ▪ Tokyo ▪ Toronto

To my wife, Linda;
my brother, Jack;
and my parents,
for their long-standing support.

International Marine
A Division of The **McGraw-Hill** *Companies*

10 9 8 7 6 5 4 3 2 1

Copyright © 2000 International Marine

All rights reserved. The publisher takes no responsibility for the use of any of the materials or methods described in this book, nor for the products thereof. The name "International Marine" and the International Marine logo are trademarks of The McGraw-Hill Companies. Printed in the United States of America.

Library of Congress Cataloging-in-Publication Data

Tillman, Dick, 1936–
    The complete book of laser sailing / Dick Tillman.
        p. cm.
    Rev..ed. of: Laser sailing for the 1990s. c1991.
    ISBN 0-07-135788-2 (alk. paper)
    1. Sailing. 2. Lasers (Sailboats) I. Tillman, Dick, 1936–.
Laser sailing for the 1990s. II. Title.
    GV811.T535 2000
    797.1'24—dc21   99-057608

Questions regarding the content of this book
should be addressed to
International Marine
P.O. Box 220
Camden, ME 04843
http://www.internationalmarine.com

Questions regarding the ordering of this book
should be addressed to
The McGraw-Hill Companies
Customer Service Department
P.O. Box 547
Blacklick, OH 43004
Retail customers: 1-800-262-4729

Bookstores: 1-800-722-4726
This book is printed on 70# Citation
Printed by R. R. Donnelley, Crawfordsville, IN
Design by Shannon Thomas
Production management by Janet Robbins
Edited by Jon Eaton, Alex Barnett, and Margaret Cook

Dacron, Kevlar, Mylar, Marstron, Plexiglas, Rolex, Spar Partners, Spectra, Styrofoam, Teflon, and Velcro are registered trademarks.

Sketches by Jan Adkins
All diagrams by Joseph Farnham unless otherwise noted. Diagram on page 129 courtesy Brad Dellenbaugh. Diagrams on page 40 courtesy International Laser Class Association. Photographs courtesy the author unless otherwise noted. Photo(s) on page 106 courtesy Bermuda News Bureau; pages 8 and 9 (bottom), courtesy Billy Black; page 56, courtesy Sally Branning; pages 5, 11, 12, 47 (top), 58, 61 (bottom), 65, 66, 71 (top), 75, 79, 98 (bottom), 99, 102, 103, and 123 courtesy Allan Broadribb; pages 19–20, courtesy Grant Donaldson; pages 26 and 78, courtesy Elizabeth FitzGerald; page 112, Daniel Forster; page 97 (top), courtesy Ken Hopkins; page 69, courtesy John E. Hutton Jr.; pages 9 (top) and 71 (bottom), courtesy Performance Sailcraft; page 59, courtesy *Sailors' Gazette*; page 97 (bottom photos), courtesy Fran Seidenberg; page 80, courtesy Linda Tillman; pages 17 (right), 21, and 74, courtesy Craig Van Collie; page 17 (left), courtesy John Weber; and page 6, courtesy *Yacht Racing/Cruising*.

Contents

Foreword

BRUCE KIRBY

This fourth edition of Dick Tillman's excellent book, now retitled, coincides with the Laser's 30th anniversary. The continued growth and vitality of the class is fascinating to those of us who have been there since the beginning. I am amazed to realize that most 18- to 30-year-old competitors in Laser class events were not even born then. But Masters competition, for ages 35+, has also become a major part of Laser racing, and hundreds of participants often turn out for Masters championships. Many of these sailors have stayed with the class over the years, but others have returned to the fold after forays into larger boats.

Coinciding with the spread of Masters competition has been racing with the Radial rig, and some of the largest events today are held with this reduced sailplan, which is better suited to those weighing under 150 pounds (68 kg). The Radial has also proved very popular for the recreational sailor, many of whom prefer the slightly toned down feel of the smaller rig. This diversification, which has attracted sailors from 15 to 70 years and from 125 to 200 pounds has served to stimulate the world of Laser sailing and should propel it well into the 21st century.

The two questions I'm most frequently asked about the Laser are: What has it meant to you, and what do you think it has meant to the sailing world in general?

The little boat has been a constant joy to me, not only for the obvious reason that it has generated a lot of income, and continues to do so, but perhaps more important, because it has been a joy to so many other people. Even after all these years, when I see a hundred Lasers racing I have a feeling of pleasure rather than pride, a sense of "Wow, I've helped all those people do something they really like."

And I must admit to taking great delight in watching the results of virtually all other major racing classes and reading the names of current and former Laser sailors who are winning and placing well in regattas all over the world. At the America's Cup matches, almost all the competitors are current or former Laser sailors. (Perhaps some of the muscle men on the coffee grinders don't know any more about Lasers than they do about their America's Cup boats.) Admiral's Cups and the professional match racing events are like old home weeks for Laser sailors.

When one looks back at a happy story with which one has been involved, there is a tendency to obscure the facts in a fog of zeal, and perhaps to revise the story's beginning to make it better suit what took place after. The evolution of the Laser's design from the sketchpad through the normal design process and into mass production in several countries is told in chapter 1 of this book, but how it felt to watch it all happen is quite a different story.

Before the Laser, I had designed only a few International 14s, a class in which continual development is permitted and encouraged. I had difficulty accepting that the Laser must remain unchanged. Even after the boat began selling well—even when it became clear that it would have been unwise to change the smallest detail— I fretted over such features as the sleeve sail. Could we figure a way to send the sail up and down with a halyard and still keep it simple? What about the traveler? Should the boat have midboom sheeting, which I had helped to pioneer in the International 14?

It was probably a year after the boat had been introduced when I finally realized it must be left alone. As a one-design sailor I had known that all along, but as a developmental designer I always had the urge to tinker.

In the early days, those of us close to the scene knew pretty well where every Laser was. There was a fleet growing in Lake St. Louis, west of Montreal, and groups in Connecticut, Oyster Bay (New York), and on the New Jersey Shore. One day, while driving from Montreal to Connecticut, we saw a Laser sailing on a manmade lake beside the St. Lawrence Seaway. Although it was only one boat, and was not being sailed very well at that, it was a milestone because we didn't know who owned it, where it had come from, and why it was there.

Then there was the first *major* regatta, when the Duxbury, Massachusetts, frostbite people asked the Laser class to join the season-end regatta in April of 1971. We scraped up 17 entries and had great racing in medium to brisk winds. But what sticks most firmly in my mind from that weekend is that I discovered to my amaze-

ment that a Laser is faster than a Finn on a beam reach in planing conditions. I had sailed the Finn in the '56 and '64 Olympics, was very fond of the boat, and in fact feel there is a little bit of Finn in the Laser. But when I hailed Olympic Finn sailor John Clarke between races at Duxbury and asked him to reach back and forth with me in the 15-knot wind, and we found that the Laser was consistently and clearly faster than the Finn (even with me weighing 20 pounds more than John), I began to think that this little machine had a real chance of catching on with serious racing sailors.

For many years I had in my yard a Laser with no hull number that I called "the first Legal Laser," although perhaps that's a redundancy since a Laser that isn't legal isn't a Laser. Two boats had been built from the original Laser molds before mine. The first was taken to the America's Teacup regatta, where the boat was unveiled to the public. It had no core in its hull laminate and weighed only 109 pounds—far below what later became the legal minimum. Then there was the boat built for rig testing. It didn't have quite the same structure as subsequent boats, and therefore was not *legal*, and it had a slot cut in the deck so the mast could be moved back and forth and the rake altered for testing purposes. The next boat built—in late December 1970—was the one from which all subsequent boats have been copied, and that is the boat I sailed for 18 years. It began life a tangerine color, but the sun took its toll, and for my last few regattas in that boat the color was listed as *awful orange*. It had a 0 on the sail because there was no number on the hull. The need to number hulls was realized with the next boat.

In 1989 the Mystic Seaport Museum (at Mystic, Connecticut) asked if they could be the keepers of old No. 0, and she is there today as one of the more modern boats in that wonderful collection.

When that first boat was delivered to me, it had no grabrails inside the cockpit, even though I had asked that they be installed as a means of pulling oneself back onto the boat after an accidental exodus. I took the boat to Riverside Yacht Club that winter and sailed it for an afternoon against their Sunfish fleet. On the way in from the course, in a solid northwester, one of their better sailors asked if he could switch boats with me. We made the change and I watched him settle on the weather deck and sheet in. As the Laser took off he threw his feet up to catch the edge of the lee deck, which is the method of hiking in a Sunfish, and of course there was no deck edge there. Over he went into 33°F water. He had some difficulty getting back aboard, having to reach all the way in to the hiking strap, which wasn't easy in pre-drysuit frostbite gear. He had a rather tentative sail back to the dock.

After that I had a doubly good reason for insisting on the grabrails—first to help keep you aboard, and second to help you back in when you do fall out.

Dick Tillman won our first biggie. The North American Championship was slated for the Baltimore Yacht Club in October, 1971. We had put it off until October to give the class a chance to grow, so the turnout would not be disappointing. Boats started showing up the night before the first race, and continued to arrive right up to start time. Entries passed the 50 mark on Friday night and kept climbing before race time on Saturday. We began to realize there was a strong chance that 100 boats would show up— and this was only 10 months after the first boat was sold! It didn't quite happen. Registration was in the mid-90s, and 87 boats actually raced.

But what a thrill—scores of those little hummers bouncing around Chesapeake Bay and all those people having a good time! It probably wasn't until then—two years after the boat had been designed, and a year after the first one had been built—that I finally realized something unusual was happening, and that my life was about to change dramatically.

But now that 100 boats represent only a medium-sized regatta, now that worldwide numbers are soaring toward the 175,000 mark, now that I have a house on the Connecticut shore and have sailed my own ocean racer in the Admiral's Cup, I sometimes look out the window at the turquoise Laser that has replaced the *awful orange* boat and think that, with all the doubts and self-examination that went into the design and development, it really is a dear little thing.

Introduction

DICK TILLMAN

As Bruce Kirby, the designer of the Laser, says in the Foreword to this book, the first Laser was built in late December 1970. Now, 30 years later, his "little boat" enters the 21st century as a major force in the world of sailing. But this did not happen by accident.

This is the third revision to *Laser Sailing for Beginners and Experts*, first published in 1975. That book introduced the Laser and how to sail and care for it as known in those first five years of its life. Several changes accumulated in the next five to ten years, and Dave Powlison and I teamed up to produce a second edition of the book in 1983 called *The New Laser Sailing*. By that time the class had established itself throughout the world. The Laser had been selected for the USYRU (now US SAILING) Single-Handed Championship, the U.S. and World Youth Championships, and the Pan-American Games. It had become a cornerstone of collegiate and club racing and was even being considered as an Olympic Class.

This popularity and acceptance brought a new breed of sailor to the Laser. These new sailors applied an abundance of fresh thinking to sailing the boat. They scrutinized sail trim, boat handling, boat speed, physical fitness, tactics, and strategy. They overlooked nothing, no matter how small or seemingly insignificant. All these things were examined and explained in *The New Laser Sailing* with the help of seven of the top sailors in the class at that time, each of whom wrote on a specific area of expertise.

Then, another eight years passed, with more developments in the class, new emphasis on physical fitness, and further improvements in sailing the boat. *Laser Sailing for the 1990s*, published in 1991, took the reader beyond *The New Laser Sailing* by incorporating a new interview chapter on Masters Sailing and Advanced Rigging Techniques. Other go-fast techniques remained as effective then as in the past.

So now, in the year 2000, the Laser continues to be the dominant single-handed racing boat in the world. Lasers have been counted in 120 different countries. Over 170,000 boats have been produced in five plants around the globe. It *was* selected as an Olympic Class, with the highest ever country entry represented at the 1996 Savannah Olympics. It will be in the 2000 Sydney Olympic Games as an open class for men and women. It is now seen that many of the world's top sailors perfected their skills in the Laser. The Masters Circuit (sailors over 35 years of age), established in 1980, has grown to offer big fleets and equal competition, allowing for age and physical fitness differences, for all sailors. Many of those who began sailing the Laser in the 1970s are still sailing it.

In this fourth edition, *The Complete Book of Laser Sailing*, several new interviews have been added. They explain the latest rigging and sail trimming refinements that have come into play for both Lasers and Laser Radials. There is also a new interview on women and Laser Radials, and two interviews on downwind and upwind sailing techniques. I have kept all of the original chapters, because the discussions and instructions are still applicable and many have historical interest. Some photos have been updated and each chapter has been updated to be correct for today's sailor. I leave it to you to glean all you can from the compilation of 30 years of experience from those who contributed to this book, and, through your own efforts, to achieve your personal goals in sailing the Laser.

Acknowledgments

Special thanks to the following Laser sailors and friends for their ideas and suggestions, all of which helped make this book possible: Ed Adams, Ed Baird, John Bertrand, Allan Broadribb, Carl Buchan, Luther Carpenter, Peter Commette, Brad Dellenbaugh, Libbie FitzGerald, Hans Fogh, Andy Fox, Gary Jobson, Bruce Kirby, Buzz Levinson, Tom Lihan, Andrew Menkart, Danielle Brennan Myrdal, John Myrdal, Stewart Neff, Terry Nielson, Dave Olson, Lainie Pardey, Dave Perry, Dave Powlison, Buzz Reynolds, Stuart Shadbolt, and Linda Tillman.

THE COMPLETE BOOK OF

Laser Sailing

History

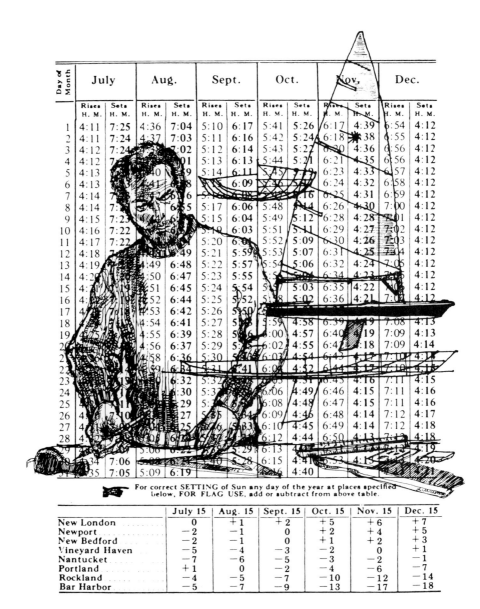

It all started with a phone call. Two top Canadian International 14 sailors, Bruce Kirby and Ian Bruce, were discussing the latter's new assignment to develop preliminary ideas for a line of camping equipment. A large Canadian retailer was behind the project, which included the possibility of a sailboat small enough to be carried atop a car.

Since Ian Bruce was an industrial engineer, he queried naval architect Kirby about designing the boat. As they talked on the phone—Bruce in Montreal and Kirby at his editorial desk at *One Design and Offshore Yachtsman* in Stamford, Connecticut—Kirby began doodling on his scratch pad. By the time the conversation was over, he held a drawing remarkably similar to what eventually became the Laser. The sketch came to be known as "the million dollar doodle."

Right from the beginning of the project, Kirby realized that the boat might never be built by the retailer who requested it. "I understood," he remembered, "that there were certain questions of marketing and so forth and that the project was somewhat tentative."

With that thought in mind, Kirby set about developing a boat that might potentially be built by someone else as a high performance dinghy. Although the boat was small, Kirby's design process was anything but simple.

"It's surprising what you have to do if you're conscientious," he said. "The big thing with the Laser was decision making. I went about the process in the same manner as if I were design-ing a half-tonner or, for that matter, an America's Cup entry. I knew I wanted no less than a 12½-foot waterline because at anything less than that, performance starts to deteriorate. But everything else was problematical."

Among the things Kirby needed to determine were the boat's displacement-length ratio, sail area, and an ideal crew weight. The latter he worked out to be some 175 to 180 pounds. He specified a hull weight of about 115 pounds, some 25 pounds lighter than a Sunfish. Working out these decisions took two or three days. Drawing the lines for the hull sections required an additional two or three days compared to the approximately two weeks Kirby spends on an IOR vessel's lines.

"The Laser," he said, "is a simple shape and that helped speed its design. That simple shape is also the boat's greatest strength."

By mid-October 1969, the basic design work was complete and the finished drawings were sent off to Ian Bruce in Canada. Soon afterwards, the firm that had requested the boat decided not to proceed with a "cartopper" after all. The plans were put in a drawer in Bruce's Quebec office. They sat there for months and, had it not been for a rather uniquely conceived sailboat race, they might have sat there indefinitely.

Early in 1970, *One Design and Offshore Yachtsman* decided to hold a regatta for boats costing under $1,000. The magazine labeled this event the *America's Teacup* and scheduled it to be held in Wisconsin that October. Kirby thought

The doodle that became the Laser. Sketched lightly beneath the boat's bow is designer Kirby's first effort at what is now the Laser's familiar, tough, hull-deck joint. At the upper left is an idea for the midship section, which remained largely unchanged as the design developed. The doodle-version Laser was equipped with a pivoting centerboard, not the production boat's daggerboard, and its transom was raked slightly rather than perpendicular. A solid gooseneck-vang arrangement is shown, but it was soon discarded as impractical. Sketched very lightly at the bottom is what Kirby calls a "first whack at the built-in bailer, later inverted to make the present recessed bailer, which now has a plastic insert to help it do the job."

The figures in the upper right corner under "DISP" are the first estimates of weights, all of which changed as the design proceeded. The simple mathematics in the middle of the sail show a calculation for area of midship section: area = displacement in cubic feet (5.4), divided by the designed waterline length (12.5) times the prismatic coefficient (.56), with the answer being 77 sq. feet.

At the top left is an effort by Kirby's daughter Kelly, then 10, to spell spinnaker. "Boycott 13," appearing at the bottom, was according to Kirby, "a nickname that Ian Bruce had back then" (1969). The doodle now hangs, framed, in Kirby's Rowayton, Connecticut, office.

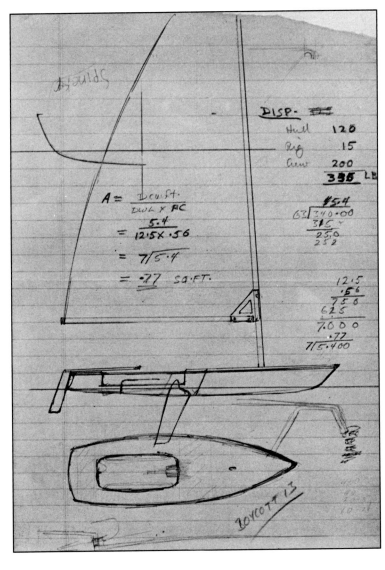

his little cartopper might make a competitive entry and he and Ian Bruce agreed to build a boat and try it out. In fact, they planned on taking a pair of boats to the race.

Kirby and Bruce turned their attention to structural details. They wanted the boat to be light yet strong and specified a foam-cored deck and a hull with foam strips on either side of the centerline. Then they devised a hull-deck joint they called a *rollover*, a curved, mated union familiar now to Laser sailors everywhere. It gives the Laser a particularly distinctive look and is so strong that the boat can be stored on its gunwale.

As work was begun on the first of what they called a Weekender, Kirby and Bruce engaged Hans Fogh to design and build the sail and skipper the boat. Fogh, an Olympic sailor and protégé of Paul Elvström's, had emigrated from Denmark to Canada in 1969. Although he had never seen the Weekender's mast, he had a sail completed by the time Bruce arrived in Toronto to pick him up and take him to the regatta. In keeping with the weekender idea of the boat, Fogh stitched the letters TGIF—thank God it's Friday—on the sail. In his first race, he placed second in class.

That night, Fogh recut the sail. "I hadn't had time to test mast bend prior to the regatta," he remembered. "I recut the luff curve to better conform to the way the mast bent. After that, the boat truly did seem fast and everybody thought we really had something going."

Fogh won his next race and was well in front in the third race when it was canceled. Back home in Canada that fall, Fogh did a lot of sail material testing. Right from the beginning of the project, he had argued for the selection of a good quality 3.2-ounce sailcloth. "I wanted good quality cloth because I knew that it could be economical if sales volume was high," he said. "I've never had any regrets about that decision. I think that it would be hard to design a better Laser sail starting from scratch today."

The tests of the boat conducted that November involved more than the sail. A second boat was finally completed and experiments were made with mast position and rake. An ideal boom was decided upon and the mast sections were finalized in December 1970. Then, a third boat was built. It was the first production version and it is still owned by Bruce Kirby. A second

Left: Designer Bruce Kirby, born in Ottawa, Canada, in 1929, grew up sailing and racing. He competed in the 1956 and 1964 Olympics in the Finn dinghy. He began his career as a newspaperman in Canada and later became editor of *One Design and Offshore Yachtsman*, now *Sailing World*. The Laser's success permitted him gradually to move into yacht design full time. He has designed over 60 boats, among which are the San Juan 24, the Sonar, a Canadian entry for the 1983 and 1987 America's Cups, and several IOR ocean racers and cruising boats. His most recent design, the Ideal 18, was a nominee for Boat of the Year in 1990. **Right:** Ian Bruce. Along with Bruce Kirby, part of the team responsible for the creation of the Laser.

production model was completed in time for the New York Boat Show in January. There, the dark green hull attracted a lot of attention and 144 orders were taken. Kirby now turned his efforts towards promoting the boat, helping to recruit dealers, and writing ad copy.

By then, the boat's name had been changed from Weekender to Laser. The precise details of the boat's name selection are rather hazy, now. Kirby's wife, Margo, remembers that she and her husband spent hours looking in a thesaurus and dictionaries and found nothing suitable. It was at a party in Montreal after the boat's design had been finalized that a science student from McGill University suggested the boat be given what Kirby recalls as "a modern, scientific name." Either the student or Ian Bruce continued the idea to its conclusion—Laser. The name impressed everybody, but Kirby wondered if enough people knew what a laser was. When his daughter Kelly, then 10, said she was studying lasers in school, Kirby lost any doubts. Ian Bruce looked up the international symbol for lasers at the McGill library and that replaced TGIF on the boat's sail. The Weekender was now the Laser.

"It took us a few months before we realized just how good a name it really was," remembers Margo Kirby.

The rest, as they say, is history. To date, over 170,000 Lasers have been sold and production has run as high as 12,000 boats per year. Because it did not prove practical to build the relatively low cost boats in Canada and then ship them all over the world, subsidiaries have been established and licenses sold by the boat's original manufacturer, Performance Sailcraft, located in Quebec. Boats are now manufactured in Australia, Chile, England, Japan, and the United States. All of the boats are built from molds made from original plugs that are maintained

The Laser prototype: at the time it was named the Weekender, the reason sailmaker Hans Fogh used TGIF as an insignia.

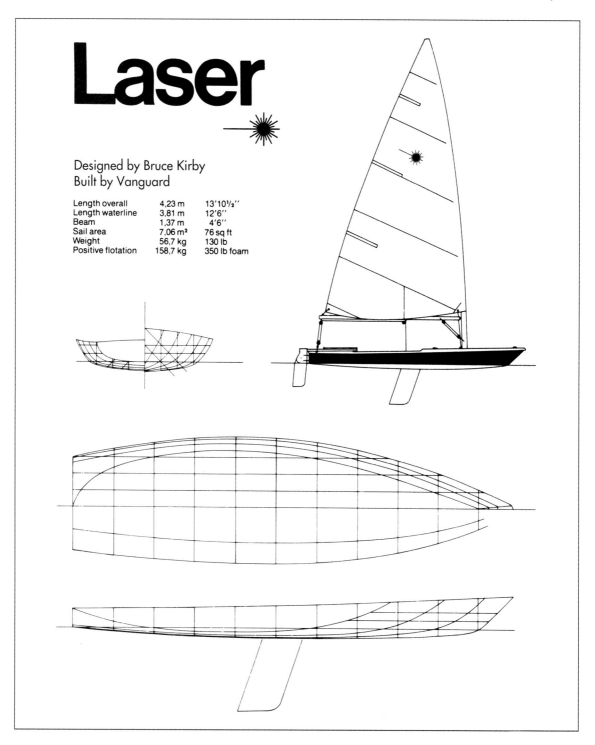

Laser

Designed by Bruce Kirby
Built by Vanguard

Length overall	4,23 m	13'10½''
Length waterline	3,81 m	12'6''
Beam	1,37 m	4'6''
Sail area	7,06 m²	76 sq ft
Weight	56,7 kg	130 lb
Positive flotation	158,7 kg	350 lb foam

Lines and sailplan of the production Laser.

according to procedures spelled out by the builders and the Class Association in a joint agreement.

With this many builders, it's important to maintain consistent quality throughout, and that is achieved through careful monitoring of each stage of construction. The builders and the Class maintain a construction manual that details each bit of material and procedure that goes into producing a Laser. The Class, the builders, and the designer all contributed to the creation and the execution of this document. The Class Measurer executes a regular audit within each factory on a periodic basis to check the adherence to the specific details of the Construction Manual.

Laser sails are manufactured under the same stringent requirements as the boats. There are currently two lofts worldwide producing the sails. The cloth, patterns, and procedures are strictly controlled by the Construction Manual.

Again, adherence to this is checked regularly by the ILCA Measurer.

The deck and hull molds are built separately, and it takes about eight hours from the time work is first started until the hardened and cured deck or hull is pulled from the mold. The

Building the Laser: (1) Laser production line in Portsmouth, R.I. (2) Resin-impregnated cloth is squeegeed to eliminate voids or bubbles. (3) A newly molded deck is joined to the hull. (4) Lasers (background) await shipment.

first step for each is to spray the mold with a layer of gelcoat, which becomes the skin of the Laser and gives it its color. Once dry, the hull is covered with a layer of four-ounce chop-strand fiberglass mat. Then PVC foam stringers are added for stiffness, followed by a layer of one-ounce mat. On the deck, a two-ounce layer of chop-strand fiberglass mat is put over the gelcoat, followed by a thick polyurethane foam sandwich. That is sealed with a one-ounce layer of mat. In addition, wherever fittings will be attached, a block of marine plywood is installed for added strength.

During the next eight-hour shift, the hull and deck are glued together and the fittings are installed. Once done, the boat undergoes a rigorous inspection of the glue bonds, each fitting screw, and gelcoat, as well as centerboard and rudder position. Even the mast rake is checked by putting a lower section in the mast step and fitting a template to it to determine whether it is within the class tolerances.

Other than the sails, the only major Laser parts not made at the factory are the spars, centerboards, and rudders. The centerboards and rudders are made of injection-molded, closed cell polyurethane with steel reinforcement rods

inside. Closed cell foam cannot absorb water. The spars are all extruded aluminum, and are made to very close tolerances. Each section is inspected as it enters the factory for proper wall thickness, diameter, and hardness. If there is any variation in those dimensions, particularly wall thickness or hardness, a spar might break, and is therefore not acceptable.

Today's Laser has changed little from the first production model back in 1971. Any changes that have been made make the boat easier to maintain, more durable, or less expensive. For instance, some wooden parts, such as the cockpit handrails, are now made of plastic, eliminating the need to varnish them every season. Older boats carry flotation in the form of Styrofoam blocks inside the hull; today's Lasers carry flexible, air-filled polyethylene containers, which are less prone to absorb moisture. However, nothing has been done to alter the Laser's performance. In the selection of equipment, the main criterion for change has always been improving function, durability, and reliability.

Three alternatives to the standard rig have come into play. With its 76 square feet of sail, the boat can become a handful for smaller sailors in a breeze—just when the going gets to be really fun. As a result, the Laser M, standing for Modified Rig, was introduced in 1975. The M rig used the standard lower mast section with a shorter upper section, reducing the sail area to 60 square feet. Ironically, even though the sail was smaller, it remained relatively powerful because of the stiff, full-length lower mast section. Furthermore, that same stiffness led to a lee helm since the mast could not easily be bent to move the center of effort aft. The M rig proved unpopular. Something better was needed to meet the requirements of Laser sailors in the 110- to 140-pound category. Thus the design of the Laser Radial Rig.

The Laser Radial rig was developed by Hans Fogh to provide still more control and performance than the Laser M. Named because of its radially cut sail in which the panels radiate up from the clew towards the luff, rather than be-

ing horizontally cut, the Radial's sail measures 62 square feet. The Radial sail is more resistant to stretch, particularly along the leech. But what really separates the Radial rig from the M rig is that instead of shortening the mast's top section to fit the smaller sail, the bottom section has been shortened and features a thinner wall to allow more mast bend. The result is a more flexible spar that allows the mast to be bent and the center of effort to move aft.

"With the Radial," said Fogh, "you can trim the sheet and free the leech and gain better balance as you hike out to keep the boat flat. In 18 knots of wind, a Radial with a lighter person can go upwind faster than with a regular sail, and, in fact, as fast as a heavier person with the full-size rig."

The third alternative, developed in 1989, is the Laser 4.7, meaning 4.7 square meters. This is the smallest of the three rigs and has a sail area of 51 square feet. It was designed to extend the range and appeal of the Laser to the much younger and lighter sailor of 75 to 120 pounds. The 4.7-square-meter sail is roughly one-third smaller than the standard Laser sail and uses a specially designed lower mast section that is pre-bent at a precise angle to recreate the exact center of effort of the standard rig. This insures that the 4.7 has the same feel and responsiveness as the standard Laser. This more manageable sail and rig is designed to allow the young sailors, as they grow in size and ability, to move up to the Radial and, ultimately, the full rig and still use the same boat.

The whole question of heavy air sailing is rather central to the Laser since the boat is so exciting when the wind is strong. In fact, the world-renowned Laser Heavy Air Slalom was created just to take advantage of this aspect of the Laser's performance. Held in San Francisco Bay, the slalom is always scheduled for what the organizers hope will be the summer's windiest weekend. The event consists of a double-elimination series in which Lasers square off against each other, one-on-one, much the way professional ski racers do. The boats tack upwind through a series of buoys, switch sides, then make a breathtaking run jibing around the buoys as they go. With the wind often in excess of 25 to 30 knots, jibing and tacking every five or 10 seconds becomes a real test of skill for the sailors, not to mention being a delight for spectators.

The now defunct Sir Francis Chichester Regatta was another event existing primarily to permit Lasers to show off in heavy going. The race involved a 70-mile heavy air reach sailed by junior sailors from the St. Francis Yacht Club on San Francisco Bay's east shore. As many as 100 Lasers used to enter the regatta during the seven years it was held.

Much of the Laser's reputation rests firmly on its ability to be sailed when other boats can't be. World-class dinghy sailor and collegiate sailing coach Skip Whyte, who has been sailing Lasers since their debut, recalled a special regatta once held in December in Rhode Island. "A big storm was forecast," he said, "and it arrived right on schedule, blowing about 50 knots or so. And a bunch of us went out sailing in Lasers in this tremendous amount of wind. We just went bombing around, having a great time. But the boats were just amazing. They're not perfect in heavy air, but they are certainly well balanced, and they don't come unglued in a breeze. I think even a light person can learn to sail the boat in a heavy wind in any direction—given the right technique. Some boats will simply stop sailing in those conditions, but that's not really a problem with the Laser."

That sentiment is constantly repeated. Said one recreational sailor, "the harder it blows, the more fun it gets. My wife feels the same way. The only reason she ever goes out in the Laser is because it's blowing like stink, and she reaches back and forth on the lake, just going fast."

The Laser Radial is an alternative rig for lighter sailors in the 110- to 140-pound range. The radial-cut sail has panels which radiate up from the clew rather than being horizontally cut.

With an original price tag of $695, a good part of the Laser's appeal was low cost. Said Whyte, "In terms of what young people are able to achieve, the Laser has opened up all kinds of horizons, mainly because it has provided a boat with good one-design characteristics with an affordable price. Overall, the boat's effect on the sport has been dramatic—everyone has seen how a group of good Laser sailors has jumped into the Finn class and totally dominated it. The Laser has helped revolutionize one-design sailing."

Gary Jobson, tactician aboard *Courageous* when she successfully defended the America's Cup, echoed Whyte's feelings. "Laser sailing," he said, "has probably drawn more people into the national and international sailing scene where they probably would not have been without that boat. There are just so many good events that a lot of people have been encouraged to pack up and go to them. It's also made a lot of junior sailors stay with the sport. They don't just quit at age 16; they keep going because there's always something else to shoot for. Plus, it gives them a chance to sail on their own rather than spending every Saturday floating around as a foredeck hand aboard someone else's 33-footer."

No matter where you go, if you are around water, you will probably find someone sailing a Laser. If there are more than a couple of them, it's likely you'll find them racing. You'll find such pockets of racing almost everywhere, from the smallest, most out-of-the-way lakes of northern New England to mountain lakes in South America. Move toward the larger population centers, and the number of boats racing increases dramatically until you begin coming across weekend regattas attracting close to 100 boats. And when the major championships roll around, boats filter in from all corners, often swelling the fleet to over 200 boats.

The Laser was named an International Class in 1974, which made it eligible for consideration as an Olympic Class. In 1994 the International Sailing Federation (ISAF), selected it as the open (men and women) single-handed class for the 1996 Olympic Games in Atlanta, Georgia, with the sailing events taking place in Savannah. The Laser was also selected for the 2000 Sydney Olympics and is expected to continue the distinction of being named as an

Olympic Class. Because of its popularity, individual nations must now qualify through competition to enter a team in the event.

The Laser Radial was introduced in 1989, providing a smaller rig on the same hull for lighter weight crew. Since it's introduction, it has proved to be as popular as the Standard Laser. Many countries are now using the Radial rig exclusively for youth single-handed sailing as an introduction to the standard rig. In 1999 there were over 300 entries from 35 countries in the Laser Radial Youth World Championship.

At the other end of the scale, the Laser class has an active Masters racing fleet (sailors over the age of 35). At the 1999 Laser Masters World Championship, 250 sailors took part in five categories. Masters sailing takes place in the standard rig for Apprentice Masters (35 to 44 years), Masters (45 to 54 years), and Grand Masters (55+ years). Great Grand Masters (65+ years), Women, and Open (35+ years) sail in the Radial rig.

Regardless of all these categories, we're talking about a simple, little boat. Let's continue by getting into the basics of Laser sailing.

TWO

Basics of Laser Sailing

HIGH & LOW WATER AT BOSTON

Day of Month	Day of Week	MARCH						Day of Month	Day of Week	APRIL					
		HIGH				LOW				HIGH				LOW	
		a.m.	Ht.	p.m.	Ht.	a.m.	p.m.			a.m.	Ht.	p.m.	Ht.	a.m.	p.m.
1	S	11 03	9.8	11 26	9.2	4 46	5 13	1	T	11 51	9.5	....	....	5 38	5 57
2	S	11 40	9.8	....	....	5 26	5 49	2	W	12 07	9.7	12 29	9.4	6 17	6 34
3	M	12 02	9.3	12 17	9.7	6 04	6 26	3	T	12 44	9.7	1 07	9.3	6 55	7 11
4	T	12 39	9.4	12 55	9.6	6 44	7 04	4	F	1 21	9.7	1 48	9.1	7 37	7 51
5	W	1 16	9.4	1 34	9.3	7 24	7 43	5	S	2 02	9.6	2 30	8.8	8 20	8 33
6	T	1 53	9.3	2 15	9.0	8 04	8 22	6	S	2 45	9.5	3 18	8.6	9 07	9 21
7	F	2 33	9.2	2 59	8.7	8 48	9 05	7	M	3 34	9.4	4 11	8.5	9 58	10 14
8	S	3 18	9.1	3 45	8.4	9 36	9 53	8	T	4 27	9.3	5 07	8.5	10 5	11 1
9	S	4 05	9.0	4			10 43	9	W	5 25	9.4	6 04	8.7	11 53	....
10	M	4 58	9.0				11 41	10		6 26	9.7	7 04	9.1	12 14	
11	T	5 55	9.2				12 23	11		26	10.0	8 02	9.8	1 15	1 5
12	W	6 55	9.			21		12			10.5	8 58	10.4	2 13	2 45
13	T	7 52	10	8 28	9.		18	13			10.9	9 51	11.1	3 11	3 38
14	F	8 48	1	9 22	9.9	2 3	11	14			11.2	10 42	11.6	4 04	4 28
15	S	9 43				03	11	15		10	11.3	11 32	11.8	4 57	5 18
16	S	10 37	11			4 53	16	16	W			12 01	11.2	5 47	6 07
17	M	11 29	11				5 42	17	T	1.8		12	.8		57
18	T	....	....	12		07	6 31	T		11.6				40
19	W	12 45	11.6				8 12		S		11.			47	9 35
20							8 12							8.8	10 14	10
21	F	28	1	3 0	10						9.4	5 34	8.5	11	
22			10.6	58			91		W	5 53	9.0	6 34	8.4		
23				6 0	8.4			24	M	6 53	9.0	7			
24	M		9.2	7 06	8.3	12 05	12 47	25		7 49					
29	S	36	9.	10 56	9.4	4 21	4 43				10				
31	M		9.5	11 31	9.6	5 01	5 19								

Average Rise and Fall 9½ feet.

When high tides exceed 9.5 feet, low tides will be correspondingly lower.

Since there is a high degree of correlation between the height of High Water and the velocities of the Flood and Ebb Currents for that same day, we offer a rough rule of thumb for estimating the current velocities, for ALL the Current Charts and Diagrams in this book.

Refer to Boston High Water. If the height of High Water is 11.0' or over, use the Current Chart velocities as shown. When the height is 10.5', subtract 10%; at 10.0', subtract 20%; at 9.0', 30%; at 8.0', 40%; below 7.5', 50%.

One of the most exciting experiences a sailor can have is his or her first sail in a new boat. This is particularly true of the Laser, for even the most experienced sailor will feel the exciting challenge of the boat from the first moment aboard. But whether you are a recreational sailor or veteran racer, take the Laser out for your first sail in light to moderate winds—6 to 10 knots—and smooth water. Under those conditions, you can easily and safely become familiar with the boat's few but essential controls while still enjoying its unique responsiveness. If conditions are rough, you will probably be so busy simply keeping the boat under control that you may capsize before you have figured everything out.

Sailing the Laser for the first time is, in principle, no different from sailing any other dinghy. The most striking aspect of the boat is its pleasant sensitivity to sail trim, tiller movements, and weight positioning. Everything you do should be done smoothly and gently, at least until you develop a good feel for the boat.

Upwind, basic technique demands that the sail is trimmed in fairly tightly and the boat is sailed flat. If it is windy enough to require hiking, be sure the hiking strap is adjusted so that you can hike out in relative comfort. If you experiment with different mainsheet adjustments, you'll soon feel the boat come to life and you'll fall into the groove where all is in perfect balance. If the wind picks up to the point where you can no longer keep the boat from heeling too much by

hiking out and trimming the sheet, try raising the daggerboard five or six inches. That, coupled with quickly easing the mainsheet in the puffs and then trimming back in once the puff has passed, should reduce the angle of heel.

Sailing offwind in a Laser for the first time can provide some of the most thrilling moments afloat, especially on breezy reaches. As when going to windward, the Laser performs best offwind when kept flat on its bottom. Pull the board one-third of the way up on reaches and runs. Then keep adjusting the sail as the wind direction shifts.

Be careful not to let the boom drag in the water, as it can easily turn your fast reach into a fast swim. If it is dragging, flatten the boat by hiking a little harder. If you find the bow is starting to dig into the waves, slide aft as far as possible. In very heavy wind, you may have to slide so far aft that only your calves and feet are in the cockpit. It may seem like a fairly awkward position, but the control and speed you gain in doing so will be well worth it. It doesn't take much to pop the lightweight hull up onto a wet and thrilling plane. And, by keeping the boat properly trimmed, you can maintain a plane for a considerable distance, blasting over the waves on a ride you will long remember.

There is one point of sail where the Laser is especially sensitive—dead downwind in winds over 10 knots. In these conditions, it is possible to let the sail out so far that the boat

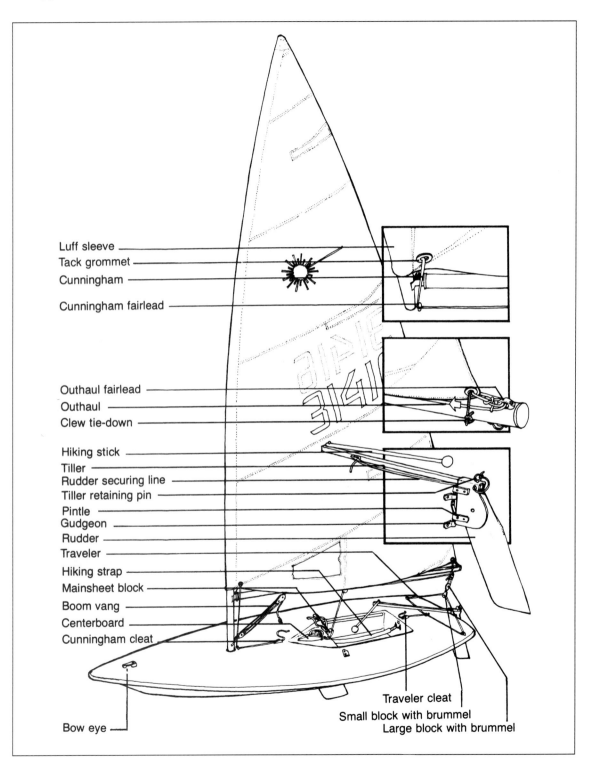

Luff sleeve
Tack grommet
Cunningham
Cunningham fairlead

Outhaul fairlead
Outhaul
Clew tie-down

Hiking stick
Tiller
Rudder securing line
Tiller retaining pin
Pintle
Gudgeon
Rudder
Traveler
Hiking strap
Mainsheet block
Boom vang
Centerboard
Cunningham cleat

Traveler cleat
Small block with brummel
Large block with brummel

Bow eye

begins oscillating—heeling first to windward, then to leeward. If left unchecked, these oscillations will eventually result in a capsize to windward, commonly referred to as a *death roll*.

To prevent a death roll, first try lowering the board all the way. If the oscillations continue, make sure the vang is set tight, then trim the mainsheet several feet. One or more of these techniques should considerably lessen, or eliminate, the oscillations in all but the strongest winds. Then, you must supplement these techniques by sharply trimming the sheet each time the boat starts heeling to windward. Even if only trimmed a foot or so, the effect of this trimming will immediately pull the boat back to a vertical position.

Tacking

The most valuable Laser sailing skill is proper tacking. No matter what the wind speed, you must only attempt to tack when the boat is moving well. Because of its light weight, the Laser carries very little momentum. A tack attempted from a near stop will almost always leave the boat in irons. This is particularly true in winds over 10 knots.

Let's examine tacking, step by step. Assume you are on a starboard tack and sitting on the windward side within the front third of the cockpit. The sheet should be pulled in tight, with the boom just over the leeward transom corner. Your shoulders are parallel to the gunwale. You should

Left: Prepare to jibe! As soon as Laser 55612's boom crosses the cockpit during the jibe, the helmsman immediately works to get the boat level. Once he has accomplished that, all he will need to do is switch hands on the tiller and mainsheet. **Right:** A time-wasting predicament that can lead to a capsize: here in mid-jibe, the wind is coming over the port quarter but the sail is still on the port side of the boat—sailing *by the lee*. As soon as you reach this point, grab the mainsheet just below the block on the boom and give a quick tug to start the boom over. The helmsman pictured could have avoided his predicament if he had started the boom over earlier.

have the tiller extension in your left hand, holding it with your palm down and your hand close to your chest. The mainsheet is in your right hand, with the sheet coming in under your little finger and your thumb is up.

STEP 1. With the boat up to speed, initiate the tack by pushing the tiller extension slowly and smoothly to leeward with your left hand. At the same time, your right hand should be easing the sheet a foot or two. Begin to turn your body, facing forward.

STEP 2. As you turn, holding the tiller extension near the long end, twist your left arm behind you, bringing the back of your hand close to the small of your back. As you complete your turn, slide onto the port deck (new windward side), still holding the tiller extension behind your back with your left hand, and the sheet in your right hand.

STEP 3. Now, trim in the sheet a foot or two with your right hand by pulling it aft toward the tiller extension, which you are still holding behind your back in your left hand. Grab the tiller extension with your right hand and momentarily hold it and the sheet in one grasp. Now let go of the tiller extension with your left hand, freeing it to take hold of the sheet where it exits the mainsheet block in the center of the cockpit. Release the slack sheet from your right hand grasp while maintaining control of the tiller extension. Pivot the tiller extension across the front of your body and hike out. You are now on port tack.

Tacking from port to starboard is identical, except for using opposite hands. Practice both tacks repeatedly and this important technique will soon feel natural. This behind the back tacking technique applies to all small boats fitted with a tiller and extension. The tiller and extension should ideally be long enough to just reach the center-mounted mainsheet block when they are fully extended toward the center of the cockpit.

Jibing

The keys to a successful basic Laser jibe are keeping the boat flat throughout the maneuver and preventing the mainsheet from getting snagged on the transom corner. Let's now examine jibing, step by step. Assume you are running on starboard tack and are sitting on the starboard side of the cockpit, facing forward, tiller extension in your left hand, sheet in your right. In preparation for the jibe, make sure the board is halfway up. This provides a pivot point for the boat, yet does not provide so much resistance that the boat *trips* during the jibe—an almost certain capsize situation. If the mainsheet is all the way out, bring it in two or three feet so that the boom is not beyond perpendicular (90 degrees) to the boat.

Now, making sure the boat is up to speed, continue using your body to keep the boat flat. Bring the tiller smoothly toward you and the boat will begin to bear off. Move to the center of the cockpit, or even to the leeward side of the boat, if necessary, to keep the boat level. As in tacking, face forward as you cross the boat during the jibe, and use the same method for switching hands on the tiller extension and sheet.

As the boat bears off, there will be a short moment when you will be sailing *by the lee*. In other words, the wind will be coming slightly over the port quarter, yet the sail will still be on the port side of the boat. Once by the lee, grab the mainsheet just below the block on the boom and give it a quick tug. This starts the boom across. Once it starts across, but before it gets directly over the boat, give the mainsheet a second sharp tug. This flips the sheet just enough to prevent it from snagging on the transom corner.

As the boom swings across, duck, slide to port and, if you haven't done so already, *quickly* return the tiller to amidships or beyond to bring the boat back to the desired course. With the jibe now completed, you should be sitting on the port edge of the cockpit, running on port tack.

Capsizing

Whether a beginner or expert, sooner or later you will capsize. If you do, don't be alarmed. Righting the Laser is simple. Make sure the mainsheet is loose. Then put your weight on the board and the boat should come right up. To provide maximum leverage when righting the Laser, especially if you are a lightweight, make sure the board is all the way down.

If you have capsized in fairly windy conditions, it is important to swing the bow of the boat into the wind before attempting to right it. This can be accomplished by hanging off the bow while in the water, thus using your body as an anchor around which the boat will pivot, or by

With anticipation and agility, you can perform a fast—and dry—capsize recovery. (1) Capsize begins. (2) As soon as you know the boat is going over, lean back onto the windward gunwale.

(continued next page)

(continued from previous page)
(3) Swing one leg over the gunwale and stand on the centerboard. **(4)** Put your hands on the gunwale and step backwards on the board to apply leverage. **(5)** Climb back onboard.

actually swimming the bow into the wind. In either case, be sure you have a life jacket on. Once the boat is positioned so that the bow is facing into the wind, you should be able to easily pull the boat back up without having it tip back over again once you've raised it.

If the boat capsizes so that the mast is pointing straight down—a *turtled* position—you must first climb up on the overturned hull. Be careful, as it will be wet and very slippery. Then, for maximum leverage, pull the board all the way up. Next, with the wind at your back, stand on the bottom of the boat's windward rail and grab the board as high as you can; lean back and pull. The Laser should come right up. If it appears reluctant, double check to make sure the sheet is loose, then give the board a few careful but strong tugs. Remember, even with the sheet loose, you are fighting a lot of resistance created by an entire Laser sail, mast, and boom being pulled up through the water. It may take a few moments to right the boat from a turtled position.

Docking and Landing

To approach a dock or otherwise land the Laser, go slowly! Point the boat into the wind as much as possible. If this is not possible, take out the figure-eight stopper knot at the end of the sheet where it goes through the block at the centerboard. As you approach your landing, let the sheet run through the blocks. This allows the boom to go out in front of the boat and you can then slowly drift in. Step out of the boat, take the boom off and remove the mast with the sail on it, laying the rig down out of the way.

Rigging the Laser

Although the Laser is one of the simplest boats to rig, it is important to learn the function and purpose of each part. Especially for new sailors, it will be helpful to study the drawing on page 16 with the labeled parts as those parts will be referred to in this book.

You may notice some variation in the way different Laser sailors rig their boats, particularly between recreational sailors and racers. Even though the setup may look different, the basic principles remain the same. The goal is to make sure everything functions properly. For recreational sailors, this helps ensure a safe and pleasurable time in the Laser. Especially if you are setting the boat up for the first time, be sure to follow the directions carefully.

Reefing

Occasionally you may run into conditions so severe that no matter how good your technique,

A properly reefed Laser sail: the size of the sail can be reduced by rotating the mast and continually wrapping the sail around it. Two to three is the minimal number of wraps: one turn around the mast only tightens the leech without significantly reducing sail area. For three turns, the top batten has to be removed.

Top: Setting up the Laser: place the sleeve of the sail onto the mast, taking care to see that the cunningham grommet is on the same side as the gooseneck. Lift the mast vertically and place it gently into the mast step after checking to see that the step is free of grit or dirt. At the stern, the traveler has been rigged through its fairleads to the traveler cleat.

Bottom: To rig the cunningham, leaving a three-foot tail, tie a clove hitch around the vang tang, leaving the tang's hole exposed. The vang swivel should already be attached to this tang. Tie a bowline in the end of the tail. Thread the bowline through the cunningham grommet of the sail.

Pass the longer tail up through the bowline and back down through the fairlead close to the mast step, then aft into the cleat. Tie a bowline in the end of the line with a loop large enough for your hand.

The outhaul is now being rigged. Tie the bitter end of the outhaul to the plastic fairlead on the outboard end of the boom and thread the outhaul through the clew grommet in the sail and back through the fairlead. Then lead it forward to the cleat on the top of the boom. Tighten it enough so that it will keep the boom on the gooseneck pin, and tie a large bowline in the end of the line to make it easy to grab.

you are simply overpowered. At these times, you might consider reefing the sail. Reefing should be particularly appealing to anyone weighing less than 150 pounds who finds the boat overpowered in winds over 20 knots.

To reef the Laser sail, first pull the cunningham as tight as you can; pull the cunningham grommet down so that it is almost touching the gooseneck fitting. Instead of leading the cunningham line down through the deck fairlead, as usual, tie it off on the mast-mounted boom vang bail. Then with the outhaul, vang, and boom dis-connected from the mast, tightly wrap the sail around the mast two or three times. One turn only tightens the leech and does not significantly reduce sail area. For three turns, you must re-move the top batten. Then reconnect the boom, outhaul (you may need a longer outhaul line), and vang. You now have a rig that is not only con-trollable in strong winds, with no excessive helm, but one that is also responsive and seaworthy.

Obviously, by reefing you will create some sail shape distortion, but sailing with that distor-tion is often more efficient than being drastically

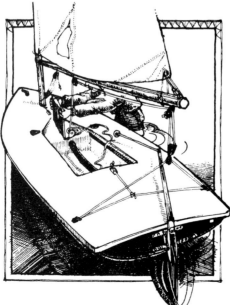

Top: With outhaul and mainsheet rigged, the rudder is about to be mounted. In the drawing below, the method of rigging the main-sheet is evident. The small block with brummel hook on the traveler has been clipped to the larger block. **Bottom:** One end of the mainsheet has been knotted onto the becket of the becket block, us-ing a figure-eight stopper knot. The sheet was then led through the large block, up again through the becket block, forward through an eyestrap on the boom to the boom block and then down through the mainsheet ratchet block in the cockpit and to the cleat. It is wise to tie a stopper knot on the sheet end to keep it from running out through the blocks accidentally. The tiller extension has been attached to the tiller which goes beneath the traveler permitting the traveler to be tightened as necessary. The outhaul has been rigged and the clew tie-down wrapped twice around the boom and the clew grommet (inside the outhaul), and secured with a square knot. It should hold the clew tight against the boom but still allow it to slide forward and aft with outhaul adjustment. With the centerboard placed in its trunk, this Laser is now ready for sailing.

overpowered, especially for lightweight sailors. You will also sacrifice some offwind performance by using a reefed sail, but that too can often be balanced out by the improved upwind performance.

The Six Sail Controls

With the boat now rigged properly, the next step is to understand the functions of the six sail controls: boom vang, cunningham, outhaul, clew tie-down, traveler, and mainsheet (see pp. 22–23). Like a well-tuned automobile engine, the Laser is easiest to handle when these controls are optimally adjusted. Although a few of the six controls are occasionally thought of as "racer-only" controls, all can make big contributions to your enjoyment and safety, even at the recreational level. A brief description of each follows. For specific recommendations about how to set each control for different conditions, see the chart.

BOOM VANG: In addition to holding the boom on the gooseneck, the boom vang—or kicker—holds the boom down when sailing offwind. If the vang is not tight enough, the sail will develop considerable twist when reaching or running; the result is that the boat will be difficult to handle. The vang should be gradually tightened as the wind increases. When tying up to the dock or leaving the boat unattended, such as on a beach, be sure to loosen the vang to keep the sail from filling and tipping the boat over.

CUNNINGHAM: The cunningham controls the fore-and-aft location of sail draft—the sail's fullness. It also holds the mast in the boat when capsized. Generally, the cunningham should be tightened when beating, thus keeping the draft appropriately forward. When sailing offwind, the cunningham can be eased, allowing the draft to move aft. Like the vang, the cunningham should be gradually tightened as the wind increases. Generally, in very strong winds, you should pull the cunningham as tight as you can get it. As you will read later, some top racers adjust the cun-

ningham differently to make fine adjustments in sail shape. To make such tightening easier, try tying a small loop in the tail of the line. In addition to acting as a handhold, the loop will also prevent the cunningham line from accidentally slipping through its cleat.

OUTHAUL: The outhaul also controls draft, but mainly in the lower part of the sail. When just starting out in the Laser, it is better to err on the "too-tight" side when adjusting the outhaul. An overly loose outhaul will make the boat heel excessively when sailing upwind. So, if you are having difficulty holding the boat flat when beating, tighten the outhaul. Like the vang and cunningham, the outhaul should be tightened as the wind increases, often to the point where the foot of the sail lies drum-tight along the boom.

CLEW TIE-DOWN: The function of the small-diameter line wrapped around the boom (twice) is to hold the clew of the sail close to the boom. Although not absolutely necessary for recreational sailing, the tie-down permits more accurate outhaul adjustment and better control over leech tension.

TRAVELER: The traveler controls the lateral plane of the sail, relative to the boat's centerline. As a rule of thumb, pull the traveler line in snug and leave it there for all but drifting conditions. Then, you might want to loosen it an inch or so to allow the traveler block to slide more easily.

MAINSHEET: Although most sailors are familiar with the mainsheet as a device for moving the sail in and out laterally, it performs a second function on the Laser. Because of the boat's flexible mast, tightening the mainsheet tensions the sail's leech, which, in turn, bends the mast. This bending movement flattens the sail. So, in breezy conditions, more control (via a flatter sail) can actually be gained by sheeting the sail in tight rather than easing the mainsheet. Of course, in a very large puff, the mainsheet may have to be eased, or dumped, very quickly, which will force a good part of the sail to luff and thus prevent a capsize.

UPWIND SAIL ADJUSTMENTS

Wind	Sheet	Traveler	Boom Vang	Cunningham	Outhaul
Drifter (0–3 knots)	8–12 inches*	medium	medium, 2-inch prebend**	loose	4 inches†
Light Wind (3–8 knots)	8–12 inches*	medium	medium, 2-inch prebend**	loose	4–6 inches†
Moderate Wind (8–12 knots)	6 inches* to two-block	medium	medium, 2–3-inch prebend**	medium	4–6 inches†
Medium Wind (12–16 knots)	two-block	tight	tight, 3–4-inch prebend**	tight	2–4 inches†
Heavy Wind (16 knots up)	two-block	very tight	very tight, 3–5-inch prebend**	very tight	0–2 inches†

*   *Distance between blocks.*

** *Prebend is the distance between the aft section of the mast and luff of the sail measured at the top of the lower section when sighting up the mast from the gooseneck to the tip of the mast.*

†   *Distance from foot of sail to boom at point of maximum draft (in chop, more draft is needed; in flat water, less draft).*

What to Wear

The Laser can be sailed in startling extremes—one day you might be ghosting along under a hot summer zephyr, the next you'll feel more like you're in a speedboat than a sailboat as each powerful gust drives you across the water. Your comfort while sailing depends heavily on clothing selection; ignore the vagaries of air and water temperature and wind speed, and you'll quickly wish you'd stayed ashore. Dress comfortably and correctly for the conditions, however, and you'll feel like staying out forever.

What you wear when sailing the Laser is largely a matter of three important factors: warmth, dryness, and weight. The goals are to stay warm when it's cool and keep from overheating on hot days. In general, dryness helps to promote warmth; if you don't stay dry on cooler days, it will invariably *seem* much colder. The weight of clothing affects your movements in the boat and can contribute to early fatigue, especially if the weight is considerable (as happens when absorbent clothing becomes saturated with water after a capsize).

The exception to the dryness-equals-warmth equation is wet suits. Since there are few occasions when Laser sailors really stay dry, sailing wet is an accepted part of Laser sailing. Wet suits have consequently come into their own as part of the standard sailing wardrobe. Wet suits are designed to fit snugly, and in the event of a capsize or heavy soaking with spray, water works its way between the inside of the suit and your skin. That thin layer of water is then heated by your body and, for the most part, will remain there and keep colder water out. So, wet suits are actually not intended to keep you warm when dry as much as they are designed to keep you warm when wet, which is when you need it most. Wet suits have additional advantages: they are not bulky, so your movement in the boat is not nearly as confined as when wearing a regular foul weather suit with layers of warm clothing underneath. Even with the thin layer of water that seeps in, wet suits stay very close to the same weight whether wet or dry. So after a capsize, you won't have to drag an extra 10 to 20 pounds of saturated clothing back onboard with you, thus avoiding a lot of unnecessary fatigue.

The most popular wet suit styles are the shorty and the Farmer John. The shorty covers the same area as a sleeveless shirt and a pair of shorts, which means good protection for the torso. The Farmer John covers roughly the same area, but instead of stopping above the knees it has legs that extend to the ankles. Shorties are more popular in southern climes, where the air and water temperatures are higher, while the Farmer John is pretty much standard in the cooler north. Few sailors wear sleeved wet suits, unless frostbiting, as they restrict movement and tire the arms.

Wet suits come in a number of weights, particularly those intended more for skin diving rather than sailing. Thicker suits (3/2 mm) are warmer, but more confining. Consequently, a thinner suit (2/1 mm) that allows good freedom of movement, yet provides plenty of warmth, has become the most popular choice. When selecting a wet suit, especially one not made specifically for sailing, make sure there is good reinforcement in the seat and backs of the legs. If not, you'll have to wear a pair of shorts or trousers over the suit to prevent the deck from chafing through when hiking. (You'll also discover that you can slide in and out much more easily by wearing something over the wet suit.) If your arms tend to get cold, wear a turtleneck or wool shirt under the wet suit and/or a spray jacket over it.

In warm weather, when the wind is not blowing hard, dress in whatever keeps you comfortable. If you are especially susceptible to sunburn, wear long cotton pants, a long-sleeved cotton shirt, sneakers, socks, and a hat. You'll be sheltered from the sun's rays, but not uncomfortable in the heat.

If you haven't sailed the Laser much in breezy conditions, you will soon discover that it doesn't take much wind to cool off a spray-soaked body. Even at 70°F (21°C), a 20-knot wind can dangerously chill and exhaust even hardy sailors. To stay warm, wear clothing that will provide a wind block between your body and the breeze. The best choice is a one-piece nylon spray suit, an item manufactured by a number of marine-wear companies. This won't keep you dry, but you will not feel the wind on your skin. Spray suits are also easy to move around in, especially when sliding in and out from a hiked position; they're also lightweight, even when wet. A foul weather suit or sweatsuit will also effectively block the breeze, but these tend to be bulkier and gain a lot of weight when wet.

If sailing conditions are at the cool end of the scale and you're uncomfortable—even with a wet suit—consider protecting your extremities, especially your head. Fifty percent of your body's heat can be lost through the head. The best bet is a knit wool stocking cap, which will keep you warm even when wet. You might also protect other extremities—feet and hands. Feet can be kept warm with wool socks and boating shoes or rubber boots. In extremely wet and cool conditions, the best choice is wet suit boots or something similar. Buy boots that have a rigid sole, and they should last indefinitely. To keep your hands warm,

A lightweight, comfortable life jacket that does not restrict your mobility is a mandatory piece of equipment. Besides acting as a safety device, a life jacket can also provide extra warmth.

especially when handling wet lines and cold metal, wear leather gloves. Thicker gloves will keep you warmer, but will restrict your movement; thinner ones will give you better dexterity, but may not be warm enough. Full-fingered sailing gloves are a good choice. The decision hinges on how active you are. If you are constantly moving around, adjusting lines and steering vigorously, you can probably get away with lighter-weight items. Wet suit gloves can be worn for cold weather sailing, but they tend to wear through quickly unless protected by a pair of leather sailing gloves. That combination, although warm, tends to be bulky and limits dexterity.

For racing sailors, comfort provided by what one wears remains an important factor, but your clothing's weight takes on additional importance since it can affect performance. Extra weight in the form of clothing is definitely not fast, especially in light air. As a result, the "standard" racing uniform for cold weather is an insulated undergarment or wet suit with a spray suit worn over it. This keeps the torso warm, protects the arms and legs from spray, and permits easy sliding in and out when hiking. In warm weather, a cotton T-shirt and sailing shorts or pants will suffice.

Standard equipment among many racers is also a good pair of hiking boots. These provide support to the foot and ankle, usually have extra padding on top of the foot for added comfort, and often have ridges on the outside of the boot where the hiking strap falls for a surer grip. If using small lines for the mainsheet and cunningham, you may also want to wear full-fingered Amora (synthetic leather) sailing gloves (they have no tips for thumb and index finger).

Finally, get into the habit of wearing a life jacket. At many regattas, the life jacket flag stays up regardless of the wind velocity. Most well-stocked marine stores now carry comfortable, lightweight life jackets. Depending on how closely yours fits, you may want to wear a T-shirt or spray jacket over it to prevent the mainsheet from snagging on a corner of the jacket during a tack or jibe.

You will be able to finalize your sailing wardrobe as you continually spend more time in the Laser. Eventually, you'll know exactly what you need to keep you warm and comfortable in different weather conditions during different times of the year. The keys are warmth, dryness, and weight. Keep them in mind when selecting clothing, and you're bound to stay comfortable.

Following is a regatta checklist that can be adjusted for your own sailing requirements:

life jacket

swimsuit/hiking pants/bicycle pants

long-sleeved shirt, T-shirts

sunglasses

visor or sun hat

sunblock

drinking water container

spray jacket or one-piece spray suit

wool stocking cap

wool sweater

polypropylene socks, polypropylene
    underwear (top and bottom)

wet suit (Farmer John or shorty)
    or dry suit

hiking boots or wet suit boots

boat shoes

sailing gloves

stopwatch

sandpaper—400 and 600 wet-or-dry
    and sanding block

liquid soap, sponge, bucket

rule book, protest flag

wind pennant

spare parts, duct tape, towel, dry
    lubricant

THREE

Boat and Equipment

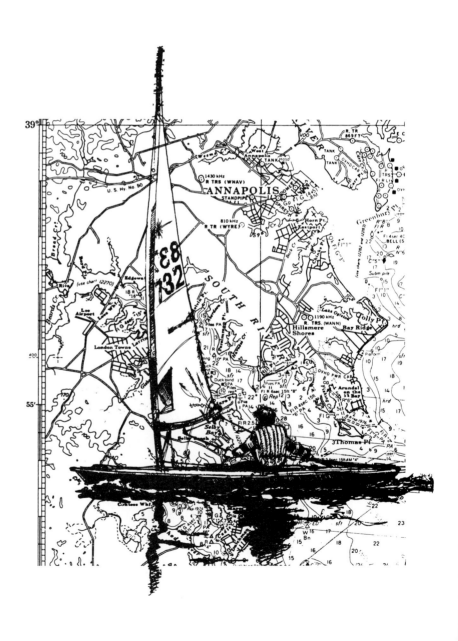

At the 1965 North American Finn Championship in Bermuda, Pete Barrett and Dick Tillman both sailed Finns supplied by the United States International Sailing Association (USISA). Both boats had bad scratches and dirt all over their hulls, which Barrett and Tillman did not have time to clean up before the first race. In that race, they finished in the top two positions, despite the rough bottoms. They then cleaned and wet sanded the hulls to make them even faster, but it did not really seem to make a lot of difference. The Laser is similar to the Finn in that there are a number of factors that affect performance, and focusing on a single detail—such as bottom finish—will by no means guarantee or deny success.

For serious Laser sailors, time spent maintaining the boat will be of little consequence if on-the-water practice time is sacrificed as a result. Any edge gained by hours of wet sanding or other similar work can be quickly lost by a few bad tacks or jibes. However, those who not only spend a lot of time in the boat, but also take detailed care of their equipment, making sure absolutely everything functions optimally, generally get the most enjoyment out of Laser sailing. And when racing, they are usually the ones who end up in front.

Although the Laser is the epitome of the one-design principle, a few minor changes can make a big difference in boat handling ease and efficiency. Most of the modifications suggested here are ideas we have seen and used at various Laser championships in recent years, and which can be made with a minimum of time and expense. Of course, none are absolutely necessary to simply have fun sailing or even perform well on the race course. However, many will allow you to more easily perform some of the techniques discussed in this book. So view them as a

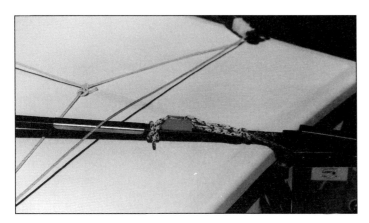

A low-profile carbon tiller with stainless steel wear strip on top. The rudder downhaul line is shown with a 2:1 purchase to hold it down securely. There is also a spacer on the top pintle to give the tiller clearance above the deck. The traveler is Kevlar with a bowline tying it together. The traveler blocks are wrapped with white duct tape to hold them straight.

list of options rather than requirements. Any one of these ideas will likely give your Laser a performance boost.

Mainsheet

The mainsheet usually has a fairly sturdy pull if you don't have a ratchet block at the aft end of the centerboard trunk. A ratchet block is now standard equipment on the Laser. However, if you have an older boat without a ratchet, you may wish to substitute the mainsheet block with a ratchet block to ease handling. The most popular ratchet blocks used aboard Lasers are produced by Harken, Ronstan, and RWO. If the ratchet is not self-swiveling, connect it to the standard eyestrap with a swivel fitting. Then, to keep the block upright, add either a spring or a few layers of tape between the eyestrap and the bottom of the ratchet block. When taping the block upright, be sure not to apply so much tape that the block no longer swivels easily. If using a spring to hold the block up, wrap one layer of tape around the outside of the spring to prevent it from snagging the mainsheet or cunningham.

Because of the emphasis in racing circles on constant mainsheet adjustment, some racers prefer not to carry mainsheet side-deck cleats. For most, however, side-deck cleats can be worth their weight, particularly in a breeze. With a number of suitable cleats on the market, two important factors to consider when making a selection are how trouble-free they will be (which is often directly proportional to the number of moving parts) and how uncomfortable they will be should you end up sitting on them (which will happen sooner or later). To mount side-deck cleats, backing plates have been molded into the underside of the deck at the front of each side of the cockpit.

The optimum mainsheet length is 44 feet—long enough to allow the boat to be sailed by the lee, when necessary. While not-so-serious racers generally opt for soft thick line, which is easy on the hands, many serious competitors prefer a waterproof line of smaller diameter, such as

Marstron line. Although it can be tough on the hands, such line does not gain weight by soaking up water and runs very easily through the blocks. The best size for waterproof, small-diameter line is $\frac{5}{16}$ inch, but ¼ inch runs through the blocks more easily in light air.

Main Traveler

The main traveler is seldom anything but bar-taut, which allows the end of the boom to be sheeted close to the aft deck. Consequently, a line that will not stretch (such as ⅛ or $\frac{3}{16}$ Kevlar) is often used to replace the standard traveler line. The newer boats come with aluminum clam cleats. If you have plastic clams, you may want to replace them with aluminum ones, which do not slip. Once the traveler is properly set, cut the tail of the traveler line off so that it is only a few inches long or tie a large loop in it. This prevents the tail from getting tangled around the hiking strap or blocking the cockpit bailer. Finally, to ensure that the brummel hooks that connect the traveler block to the mainsheet block will not bind, twist, or separate, tape them firmly together or slip a piece of plastic tubing over them. The tubing will allow you to quickly disconnect the brummel hooks, yet keep them from twisting.

Tiller and Tiller Extension

One of the most important performance factors aboard the Laser is tiller and tiller extension size. A tiller that is too long will not allow you to get back far enough in the cockpit on heavy air reaches, while a tiller extension, or hiking stick as it is often called, that is too short will not allow you to sit far enough forward in light air, perform efficient roll tacks, or hike out far enough in heavy air. A tiller extension that is of small diameter or slippery at the end where you hold it is a detriment to your sailing. A lightweight, large-diameter extension is easy to grip and less tiring to hold. The rubber universal is better than a mechanical universal as it transmits feel more directly and provides less play.

The optimum tiller length is one that comes just to the aft edge of the cockpit, which is 38 inches. The optimum length of the tiller extension is 43 inches. The combined length measured from the end of the tiller to the end of the extension when connected and extended straight with the tiller is 81 inches. At this length, the end of the tiller extension just clears the forward mainsheet block when certain wind conditions require steering without interference from the mainsheet. Longer extensions, up to 50 inches, facilitate more efficient hiking for the expert sailor but can be difficult to handle for the average sailor. The 81-inch total measurement is ideal for most.

Some of the old wood tillers may still be around. They can simply be cut to the optimum 38-inch length. They still present a slight problem in that they ride too high off the deck and create friction between the top of the tiller and the traveler line. To reduce that friction, attach a small piece of plastic, such as that from a plastic bottle, over the worn area on the top of the tiller. You can even replace the wood tiller with one that has an untapered aft end. One approach is to use a square or round piece of hollow aluminum, which is carried by most hardware stores. Such aluminum is usually untreated, so to prevent corrosion when sailing in salt water, thoroughly wash the aluminum off with fresh water after each sail. The untapered aluminum

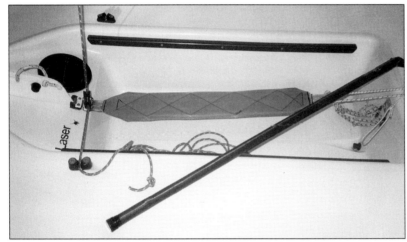

Top: This 43-inch carbon tiller extension, when mounted on a 38-inch tiller, will just clear the mainsheet block for steering. Also shown is a bungee for holding the padded hiking strap taut. The hiking strap can be adjusted using the lines shown at the aft end. The mainsheet is 44 feet long, ¼ inch in diameter. **Bottom:** Outhaul and clew tie-down: for extra purchase, rig the outhaul by tying a bowline on the outhaul fairlead, run the line through the clew grommet, or through a Harken Quick Release Hook (Harken Part No. 433) as shown in the photo, back through the fairlead, and then forward to the cleat. Notice how closely the Quick Release Hook is tied to the boom. This helps provide more control over leech tension. Use pre-stretched line wherever possible, which allows more precise adjustments in critical areas such as these. Also notice that the figure-eight stopper knot on the mainsheet is tied at the forward side of the becket on the becket block. This allows maximum block-to-block sheeting.

rides lower on the deck than the old stock wooden tillers. This creates less friction between tiller and traveler, which allows the traveler to be carried tighter and consequently allows you to sheet the main tighter, a real plus. Regardless of the type of tiller used, be sure it fits snugly in the rudder head. If there is any play, tape the aft sides of the tiller until you obtain a snug fit.

The optimum length for a tiller extension is between 42 and 44 inches, depending on tiller length. Old ski poles work well because of their light weight and relatively high strength. Another popular choice is 1-inch-diameter (or larger) PVC tubing, which is used in household plumbing. PVC tubing is particularly desirable because its flexibility eliminates breakage, and the thickness makes it comfortable to grip. Whether you use a ski pole or PVC tubing, the grip can be further improved by wrapping a few narrow layers of

marine-quality tape around the stick at intervals of 8 to 12 inches. Finally, use a swivel fitting for the tiller extension–tiller connection—one with as little play as possible as the rubber swivels. For extra strength, bolt the swivel through both the extension and tiller.

Cunningham, Outhaul, and Vang

Like the traveler and any other critical line adjustments, the cunningham, outhaul, and vang should each be rigged with line that will stretch as little as possible. For the cunningham and outhaul, use ⅛- or ³⁄₁₆-inch prestretch, or Spectron 12, 10 feet long. Use ⅛- or ³⁄₁₆-inch Spectron 12, 10 feet long, for the vang. To make sure you can easily control sail draft, particularly in heavy air, both the cunningham and outhaul can be set up

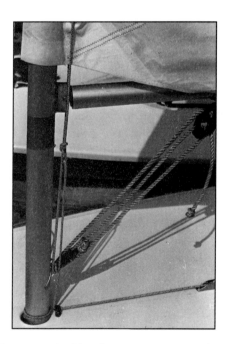

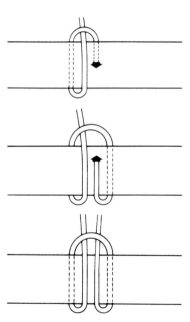

Left: An on-the-mast method for obtaining extra cunningham purchase: with 17 feet of ⅛- or ³⁄₁₆-inch Spectron 12 line, tie a lark's head knot to the vang eyestrap. Lead one end up through the sail grommet and tie a bowline at the end. Lead the other tail of the lark's head knot up through the bowline, back down through the cunningham fairlead, and finally to the cunningham cleat, making a loop for a handle at the end. **Right:** Lark's head knot, used for securing the cunningham line to the vang eyestrap for on-the-mast cunningham purchase.

with extra purchase. See chapter 11, Recent Advances in Rigging Techniques, by Dave Olson, for drawings and directions for applying multiple purchases in cunningham, outhaul, and vang.

Hiking Strap

The most important check you can make on your hiking strap is to ensure it will hold up well. Particularly if you are heavy, carefully examine all of the stitching. At the forward end, the strap will be less likely to fail if it is wrapped once around the plastic retainer located at the aft end of the top of the centerboard trunk. At the aft end of the strap, check that the screws holding the metal eyestraps to the aft end of the cockpit are tight; if in doubt, epoxy them in place. So strap length will vary only when you want it to, use prestretched line (⁵⁄₁₆-inch line is quite common) to connect the aft end of the strap to the cockpit's aft end. To make the strap easier to slip your feet under, like during a tack, take up the slack with a piece of shock cord tied between the aft end of the strap and the eyestraps at the aft end of the cockpit, or behind the traveler cleat.

If you prefer to sail barefoot, you may want to use a padded strap or slip a length of soft air-conditioning tubing over the strap, which will make it more comfortable on your feet. However, tubing tends to roll and does not provide the accurate feel obtained with just the strap and bare feet or hiking boots.

Spars

To help bend the bottom spar section when the mainsheet and vang are tightened, thus better matching the luff curve to the spar curve, the top section should fit snugly. This will ensure a smooth, curved shape to your mast rather than a V-shape, which can be caused by a loosely fitted joint. Fit can be improved by wrapping the fitting at the bottom of the upper section with package tape. Next, be sure the gooseneck bolt is tight, which ensures proper mast rotation each time the boom is eased or trimmed.

Finally, the clew and outhaul lines and sail luff will slide more easily on the spars if all sections are clean and well waxed. An even better solution is to clean them and give high-friction areas a light coating of marine silicone spray. Also, a little silicone spray or McLube in the mast step, after making sure the step is clean, will improve mast rotation. Some people use a Teflon wear strip wrapped around the mast at deck level and at the bottom.

Centerboard and Rudder

If either the centerboard or rudder "hums" while sailing, especially in planing conditions, examine the trailing edge of each blade. They should be tapered to a ¹⁄₁₆-inch thickness, with a squared-off edge. This allows passing water to leave cleanly. George Moffat writes in Stuart Walker's book, *Performance Advances in Small Boat Racing*, that squared-off trailing edges of this size are just as efficient as knife-sharp edges. In addition, they are far more durable. In any case, avoid overly thick or rounded trailing edges.

The centerboard should ride smoothly and fit snugly in the centerboard trunk. This is accomplished by adjusting the V-shaped rubber centerboard stopper (located on the deck at the aft end of the centerboard trunk) and/or by running a piece of shock cord from the centerboard's upper forward edge to the bow eye or the mast. For a handhold, to make the board easier to raise, add a rope loop handle.

On the rudder, first make certain the blade pivots forward to the maximum allowable 78 degrees. This angle is measured between the horizontal bottom edge of the aluminum rudder head and the rudder's leading edge. This assures that the rudder's center of effort is as far forward as the class rules permit, which helps reduce weather helm.

Next, make certain the rudder fits tightly in the rudder head; any play creates vibrations and sacrifices steering control. If there is play, tighten the rudder pivot bolt. If that does not eliminate play, replace the pivot bolt and its plastic bushing with a larger bolt. When using a new, larger bolt, be sure to include a lock washer or lock nut to prevent the bolt from loosening. If the tiller rubs the deck, you can put a bushing on one or both rudder pintles to raise the tiller enough for it to clear the deck.

A simple loop handle attached to the top of the centerboard makes raising the board easier. Drill two small holes as shown. Slide a fairly stiff piece of line—stiff enough to stand up on its own—through both holes and put knots at each end. Since the board is usually raised while on starboard tack (the top reach of a Laser course), the line runs from the starboard forward side to the aft port side, which makes it easier to slide your hand into the loop.

Wind Indicators

If you've practiced a lot, you will probably get to the point where you can tell by the way the boat is moving whether or not the sail is trimmed properly for each particular point of sail. But for more of a reference, several different types of wind indicators can provide considerable assistance. Shown are two types of wind indicators that can easily be attached to the mast. There are various arguments for each, and there are many other types, but in the final tally, it's a matter of personal preference.

Also, many competitors attach telltales to the mainsail to provide an indication of how the wind is flowing over the sail. They can be made of 4- to 6-inch strips of magnetic recording tape, strips of nylon spinnaker cloth, or pieces of yarn, again, depending on your personal preference. Nylon telltales fly better than wool when dry; wool flies better than nylon in rain. It helps to apply a dry lubricant, such as McLube, on the sail area around the telltales. Sailmakers recommend attaching one strip on the upper third of the sail, aft of the luff, about one-third of the distance between luff and leech. Place another strip in similar fashion on the lower third of the sail.

When sailing with telltales on the mainsail, you may encounter certain lighting conditions, such as when the sun is behind the sail, where it is difficult to distinguish between the leeward and windward telltales. To prevent such confusion, place the starboard telltales an inch or two above their corresponding port telltales. Then, all you need to remember is which telltales are the upper ones and which the lower. Telltales can also be attached to the leech of the sail.

If the sail is trimmed properly, telltales on both the windward and leeward sides of the sail will be flowing smoothly aft, as will the leech telltales. The only exception to this will be beating in medium and strong winds. Then, the weather telltales will generally be stalled out because of the higher pointing angles sailed in such conditions.

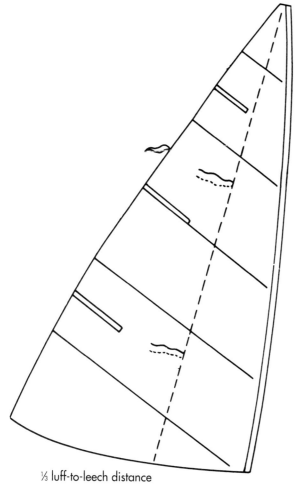

⅓ luff-to-leech distance

Wind indicators: The feather wind indicator **(1)** is attached to the lower portion of the mast with Velcro and is more in the path of your line of vision when sailing the Laser. The masthead fly **(2)** provides a wind reference at the top of the mast. Both provide valuable wind information, and your choice of wind indicator basically depends on personal preference. **Use of telltales:** Telltales positioned as indicated at left show you the way the air is flowing over the sail. When the sail is trimmed properly, the telltales on the windward and leeward sides of the sail and those on the leech will be flowing smoothly aft. If, when reaching, the leeward telltales are fluttering and not flowing smoothly, the sheet should be eased. If the windward telltales are fluttering, the sheet should be trimmed. When you are beating in medium to strong winds, the windward telltales will generally be stalled because of the higher pointing angles you sail.

Compasses

When Laser racing on small bodies of water, the shoreline can be used to check changes in headings due to wind shifts. Shoreline wind indicators—such as flagpoles and smokestacks—will provide wind direction clues. Under these circumstances, a compass is not necessary. However, if you race in open water, a good compass with easily readable numbers can be a real asset. A compass can be permanently mounted on deck or temporarily secured; a temporarily installed compass can be removed later when the boat is being stored or can be used on other boats. There are almost as many methods of installing Laser compasses as there are types of compasses suitable for Lasers. Compass selection and installation are generally a matter of personal preference. Remember, however, that class rules permit only one compass, and it may not be recessed into the deck.

Compasses and compass mounting: there are almost as many types of compasses and methods of securing them as there are Laser sailors who use them. Compasses can be temporarily or permanently secured. Class rules forbid compasses that are recessed into the deck. (1) This version is mounted on a piece of plastic with the cunningham line holding it in place. (2) Mounted on a sheet-metal base, this compass is temporarily secured by strips of Velcro glued to the deck.

(3) Compasses can be through-bolted to the deck but can get in the way when you transport the boat. To avoid this, make a plastic base for the compass, which is held in place with wing nuts. This provides a firm yet removable foundation for the instrument.

The compass should be used only as an additional source of information. Do not simply glue your eyes to it and become oblivious to all else. It takes practice and experience to use a compass effectively.

Bailer

Last, but not least, add a bailer to your boat if it does not already have one. The bailer available for the Laser is much more efficient than the standard plug arrangement. The bailer also starts working at much slower speeds. The end result is that you will never be carrying the weight of a lot of water sloshing around in the cockpit. The optional bailer also helps fair the bailer cavity, which allows water to pass more smoothly over the bottom of the hull. You must remember, however, to close the bailer before launching, as it is easily broken if it catches on anything.

From all of this information, it should be clear that the top Laser sailors are generally sticklers for detail. Perhaps that is because the class rules do not allow you to actually change the boat and, consequently, everything undergoes close scrutiny. Or, maybe this attention to detail provides more of a psychological boost: you know that absolutely everything has been thought out from every angle and that your boat is all set up in the best way possible.

FOUR

Around the Race Course

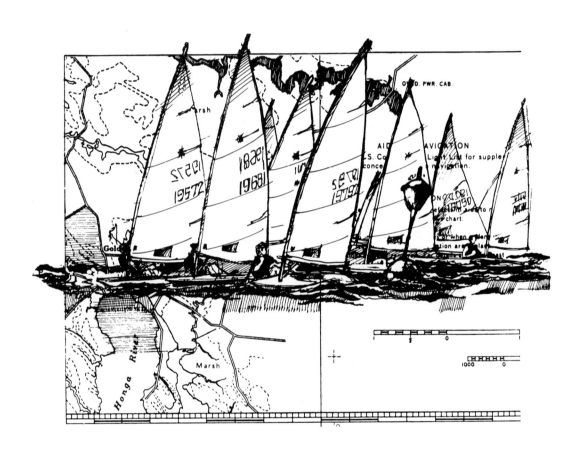

Close competition and sheer excitement draw people to Laser racing all over the world. Whether on a local, regional, national or international level, there is competitive fun for everyone. Just as there are many levels of racing, there are many ideas about how Lasers should be raced. What follows is a look at the main areas of the Laser race course and some suggestions on how to sail them. Some of the strategic and tactical thoughts expressed here represent relatively traditional ways to manage various sailing situations. Others reflect ideas that have withstood the test of time in the Laser class.

At official Laser events one of four courses is normally sailed (see diagram on page 40). Two of the standard courses are triangular (1 and 3), which provide for closer and more exciting reaches. The other two courses (2 and 4) feature only windward-leeward legs. All require starts and finishes to windward. With larger fleets, a leeward gate may be used in place of a single mark to prevent collisions.

Starting

There are a number of critical situations in Laser races that have a big effect on the outcome, but by far the most significant is the start. This is especially true in a big fleet of tough competitors. One wrong move or misjudgment at the start can easily put you over the line early or back in the second or third row of starters. Once behind, it can be very difficult to improve your position, as you will be fighting your way through disturbed wind and water created by the boats ahead.

The basics of a good Laser start are similar to those used in most other dinghy classes. At the gun, you want to be moving at top speed, be on course, have clear air, and be on the favored tack. Those things are easily said, but they take a lot of practice and experience to do effectively, particularly in a large, aggressive fleet. Let's examine the aspects of a good start, step by step.

The first key to a good Laser start is to get out to the starting area 20 to 30 minutes ahead of time and become familiar with the wind, waves and, if applicable, current. Get the boat set up properly for the conditions and get used to working it upwind. Also, begin noting the wind direction by taking compass readings on each tack. By comparing your observation or readings taken then to readings taken 10 to 15 minutes later, you may be able to detect whether there is a pattern to the way the wind is shifting, if the wind is steady, or if the wind is oscillating back and forth in a random manner.

As soon as the starting line is set, your next step is to determine which end of the line is favored. Sail down the line to about the halfway point. Then go head-to-wind, stopping the boat right on the line. If the line is square to the wind, when you are headed directly into the wind you will be in a position exactly perpendicular to the line. If the line is not square, when you are headed directly into the wind your bow will point

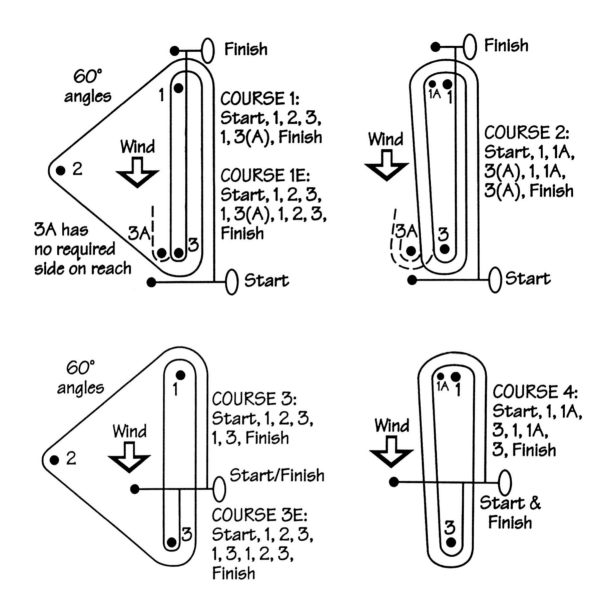

60° angles

Wind

1

2

3A

3

3A has no required side on reach

Finish

COURSE 1:
Start, 1, 2, 3,
1, 3(A), Finish

COURSE 1E:
Start, 1, 2, 3,
1, 3(A), 1, 2, 3,
Finish

Start

Wind

1A   1

3A   3

Finish

COURSE 2:
Start, 1, 1A,
3(A), 1, 1A,
3(A), Finish

Start

60° angles

Wind

1

2

3

COURSE 3:
Start, 1, 2, 3,
1, 3, Finish

Start/Finish

COURSE 3E:
Start, 1, 2, 3,
1, 3, 1, 2, 3,
Finish

Wind

1A   1

3

COURSE 4:
Start, 1, 1A,
3, 1, 1A,
3, Finish

Start & Finish

At most major Laser class events, one of the four courses shown, or some variation, is sailed. All four feature windward starts and finishes. The triangular courses are based on equilateral triangles to create exciting reaches. Course 1, known as an Olympic course, is a triangle followed by a windward-leeward-windward series (sometimes called a *sausage*). Course 1E adds an additional triangle. Courses 3 and 3E are much the same as 1, but place the start and finish line a third of the way up the wind-ward leg. This is a popular course for club racing as the race committee boat can remain on station to run additional races. With larger fleets a leeward gate (formed by 3A and 3) is used to separate boats and prevent collisions: boats heading downwind pass between 3A and 3 and then round either mark as they turn upwind. Courses 2 and 4 feature only windward-leeward legs. The windward offset, or spacer mark (mark 1A), is used with larger fleets to separate upwind and downwind traffic.

either to the pin end or committee-boat end of the line. The side to which your bow is pointing is the favored end of the line. Also note the position of the windward mark relative to your head-to-wind heading. If the mark is directly in front of you, the first leg is square. If the mark is off to either side of the bow, that side will be the quickest route to the weather mark, barring wind or water differences from one side of the course to the other.

Now take some more wind readings, either by using land bearings or a compass, and compare those readings to the ones you took earlier. Try to determine if the wind is oscillating or shifting persistently. An oscillating shift is a temporary change in wind direction. Consider, for example, a southerly breeze: an oscillating wind will vary temporarily from the constant wind direction, but the southerly direction of the wind will prevail. Oscillating shifts may or may not have a pattern to them. A persistent shift is when the wind slowly changes direction, say from southerly to southeasterly. The wind may swing 10 degrees in 10 minutes, then 10 more degrees in the next 10 minutes until it stabilizes at its new direction. If the wind is shifting persistently at the start,

you will probably want to head initially toward the direction the wind is shifting. If the wind is shifting to the right, sail to the right side of the course initially. Then, when you tack, you can tack short of the windward mark lay line so the shifting wind will gradually lift you up to it.

If the wind is oscillating, or shifting back and forth, note the range of that shifting and how long it takes the wind to shift from one direction to the other. Note the direction on your compass and keep a close eye on your watch. If those shifts do have a pattern and you can get in phase with them at the start—be at the starboard end of the line when the wind is to the right or at the port end when the wind is to the left—your start can be greatly improved. For example, consider a wind that is shifting every 15 minutes. At 10 minutes before the start, the buoy end is favored; at the 5-minute gun, the line is square to the wind. You can then conclude that, at the start, 5 minutes later, the committee-boat end will be favored. The amount it is favored will, of course, depend on the degree to which the wind is shifting.

Sometimes a shift will create a jam of boats at one end of the line. If the shift is significant—as is often the case with winds that are shifting

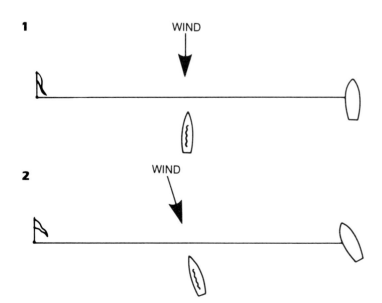

1 WIND

2 WIND

Finding the favored end of the starting line: sail right up to the line and bring your boat head-to-wind. If the line is square (1), you will be in a position perpendicular to the line when you are heading directly into the wind. If the line is not square to the wind (2), when you are headed directly into the wind, your bow will either point to the pin (buoy) or committee boat end. The end to which your bow is pointing is the favored end of the line.

persistently—you may have little choice but to join the crowd, especially if the race committee fails to notice the problem and does not reset the line. Generally, it is better to avoid tangling with the crowd, since only one or two boats out of that entire pack will end up with the perfect start. The odds of your being one of them are slim; you will probably be forced, along with the rest of the pack, to sail in disturbed wind and water, unable to tack free as quickly as you might like.

At other times the line will be square, but because of the fleet size, the line will be wall-to-wall boats by the time the starting gun goes off. Don't be afraid of trying for a front-row seat. Be prepared to get to the front and stay as close to the line as possible as early as the preparatory (five-minute) signal. Those caught behind the pack with only a minute or two before the start may find it impossible to locate a position in the front row, and even if they do, the enormous blanketing effect of the boats to windward may make it impossible to get there.

Once in the front row, your next concern is staying close to the line without crossing it, which means you must know exactly where the line is. In a big fleet where the line is particularly long, and boats at one end or the other can block your view of the buoy or the committee boat, the best method of locating the starting line is to use a *line sight*. To set up a line sight, sail off to one end of the starting line shortly before the starting sequence begins. Align the two ends of the starting line with a point on the far shore that you can easily identify, such as a clump of trees or a building. Then, sail to the opposite end of the line and follow the same procedure with the other shoreline. Now, if during the final moments in the starting sequence one end of the line becomes blocked by boats, all you have to do is line the visible end up with the line sight you have selected on the shoreline. If the point on shore is to windward of the end of the line you are sighting, you are over the starting line. If the point is to leeward, you are behind the line.

Sometimes, you will not be able to see either end of the starting line, or there will not be a shoreline visible. If that's the case, simply stay with the pack, bow-to-bow with the boats around you. That way, if the race committee sights the fleet as being right on the line or if only a few boats are over early at the ends, you will be right up front rather than buried in the pack.

Another method of getting a good start in a big fleet where the race committee has set a long line is to take advantage of midline sag. Because many competitors will not know exactly where the line is, particularly those in the middle furthest away from the reference points provided by the ends, the tendency is to hold back slightly just before the start. The result is a large dip in the middle of the line. With the aid of a line sight or simply by being aware that midline sag is a common occurrence, you can often work out a lead of a boat length or so before the gun even goes off. Begin sheeting in 10 to 15 seconds before the start, and by the time the starting gun sounds, you'll be right on the line with good boat speed and with a quick lead over those unaware of the sag.

However, in a fleet of tough competitors, the presence of midline sag should not be relied on. In fact, there may even be a bulge to the weather side of the line. In that case, you will have to concentrate on protecting your leeward side while discouraging others from driving over you. If you can position your boat so that no other boats are in the area several boat lengths to leeward, you will have room to bear off for maximum speed just before the gun. Then, a second or two before the start, head up to course, and you will come out ahead of all those around you. The best method of creating that space to leeward is to luff the boats to windward. You will be holding up those boats, and the boats to leeward will continue sailing down the line, resulting in a space, or opening, to leeward. Don't open that space up too early, as another boat may well seize that opportunity to find a front row seat. Wait until 10 to 20 seconds before the gun, then begin to create the opening.

If it appears that you may be unable to create sizable space to leeward, there are several methods to keep yourself from getting buried.

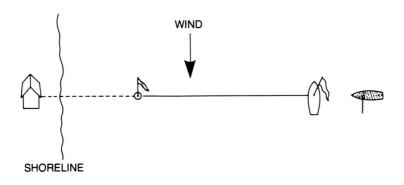

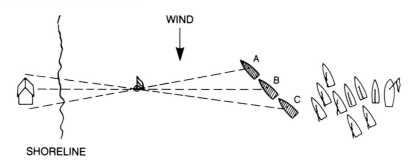

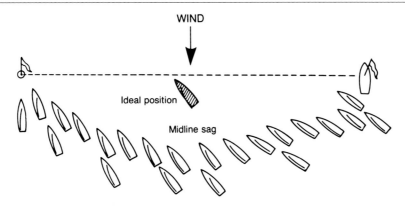

Top: Sail off to one end of the starting line and align the two ends of the line with a visible landmark on shore, such as a clump of trees or a building. **Middle:** If you are at position A at the start, when you sight down the pin your landmark will appear to windward of your line of vision. If you are at position B at the start—right on the line—your landmark will appear right in line with your line of sight on the pin end. (Remember, you do have a few feet of bow in front of you when you are sighting from the cockpit. Your bow *might* be slightly over the line.) If you are at position C at the start, when you sight down the pin your landmark will appear to leeward of your line of vision. Note: Committee boat end obscured by other boats, many of which are over the line early. **Bottom:** Midline sag: many competitors may not know the exact location of the starting line. Their tendency will be to hold back at the start to avoid crossing the line too early. The result is a large dip in the middle of the line of starters—midline sag. If you know the exact location of the starting line, you can take advantage of midline sag and establish a lead of one boat length or so before the starting gun even goes off.

Stewart Neff, a former national champion, has consistently been a good starter in the Laser class. Neff says, "I use my knowledge of the speed of various competitors in the fleet. If I know I want to start at a certain part of the line and am sure the line will be very crowded, I pick out several sailors who I know are slower than I am. I plan to start next to them with the idea that even if they do pull off a good start, I can drive over them to windward or out from under them. If I start next to someone who is exceptionally fast, or someone who can really point high, I might be the one who gets buried."

Another starting suggestion is provided by Andrew Menkart, a past North American champion. "At the start," says Menkart, "I set my sail up to provide a little extra pointing ability, which allows me to pull out from under anyone who threatens to drive over me to windward. I set my outhaul and vang as usual for the upcoming weather leg, but carry my cunningham much looser. That provides a flatter sail entry, which allows me to point higher. It also gives the sail a little more power, which I can convert into extra speed by simply sprinting, or hiking extra hard, in those critical moments right after the gun. Once the starting confusion has cleared and I am in

clear air, I retrim the cunningham to its proper position for that leg. One condition in which this technique doesn't work well is in very strong breezes. Then, when you lean in to readjust the cunningham, you lose whatever you have just gained. However, particularly in medium winds, this method can really pay off."

Menkart's planning exemplifies what one must think about when going for a good start in a tough Laser fleet. All sail adjustments should be made at least 10 seconds before the gun in medium and heavy air, and as much as 15 to 20 seconds before in light air. You will then be ready to hike and steer to get the boat moving while those who have not properly planned their starts will still be making adjustments. This factor alone can be worth at least a half a boat length.

Overall, Laser racers are probably the most aggressive sailors around, especially on the starting line. So it is absolutely vital not to give an inch before or just after the start. Don't let another boat climb over you to windward or backwind you from leeward. And, of course, try to start at the favored end of the line. If you can do these things, you can end up sailing at top speed and in clear air moments after the gun—proof of an effective start.

Big fleet start: stay close to the line and strive for a front row seat to windward. If you let yourself get to leeward of the pack, you'll have a hard time fighting your way upwind because your air will be blanketed by the many boats to windward.

Upwind

Initially, upwind success is a direct function of boat speed. However, once you have logged enough time in the boat to have maximized your speed, Laser racing becomes extremely tactical. Most of the tactics that are successful in other classes work in the Laser class as well. For instance, a standard strategy is followed by Stewart Neff: "I just try to stay with my competitors, playing the shifts and waiting for them to make the mistakes. Then, unless I'm really back in the fleet, I try to pick off the boats ahead of me, one by one."

Part of what makes the Laser such a unique tactical boat is its acute sensitivity to shifts and its capacity to quickly and efficiently respond to them. By watching the sail and being attentive to boat speed, wind shifts can be detected fairly easily. And if you need to tack away, a good roll tack will cost you virtually no ground. In oscillating winds, most follow the general rule of tacking on the headers so that you are always sailing in a lift. However, make sure you are far enough into the header before you tack. Otherwise, once you go over to the lifted tack, you may sail right out of the lift and into another header. In persistent shifts, the general rule is to always try to position yourself on the inside of the shift. That way, you'll end up lifting inside boats further to the outside, thus gaining valuable distance. If you're on the outside of a persistent shift, you'll end up sailing a long distance by following the *great circle route*.

In addition to the boat's sensitivity to wind shifts, there are usually so many Lasers on the course that the fleet can be read by carefully noting the speed and tacking angles of the other boats. For that reason, John Bertrand, two-time Laser World Champion, doesn't even use his compass on upwind legs. Instead, he prefers to watch the tacking angles of the fleet.

However, your observations about other boats' tacking angles must be accurate. Says Andrew Menkart, "Your accuracy can make a big difference in your upwind game plan. For instance, suppose there is a boat on the same tack ahead and to leeward of you. You figure that, if he tacks, he will not cross you. Then he tacks, and it appears he will cross you after all. You must now decide whether to take his stern and lose speed because of the disturbed wind and water, or tack on his lee bow, preserving your speed, but possibly being forced to the unfavored side of the course or into heavier traffic."

Knowledge of tacking angles can also play a critical role when the fleet splits—half goes to the right side of the weather leg and half goes to the left—as is often the case in big Laser fleets. In most cases, one of those two groups is going to come out ahead. Buzz Reynolds, a top Laser sailor, suggests how to deal with those situations. "I always try to delay my decision about what side to go to as long as possible by staying in the middle," says Reynolds. "Sometimes that even means sailing in slightly disturbed wind and water. Then I carefully watch the tacking angles of the two groups and will eventually detect which side is gaining. At that point, I sail to that favored side and reap the benefits." Reynolds does note some cautions about using this method: "It doesn't work too well in light air. Then, one side generally pays off much more than the other, and once you figure out which side is best, it may be impossible to get over there in time to take advantage of the shift."

Occasionally, particularly after a poor start, you may end up behind someone you believe is slower than you. It is better to take evasive action right away than be held back. The most straightforward option is to immediately tack away, but you may not want to go in the other direction. The alternative is to try and pass the slower boat either to windward or to leeward. When trying to pass to leeward, Menkart suggests, "The best time to make your move is in a puff. Quickly foot off, keeping the boat flat by hiking hard and sheeting out slightly. In addition, slide aft six inches or so to keep the bow out of the water and allow the boat to foot faster on its flatter stern sections."

If you are dead behind a slower boat, it is very difficult, if not impossible, to pass it to windward. "But," says Menkart, "if you are just to

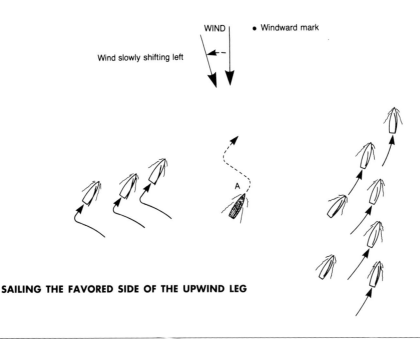

SAILING THE FAVORED SIDE OF THE UPWIND LEG

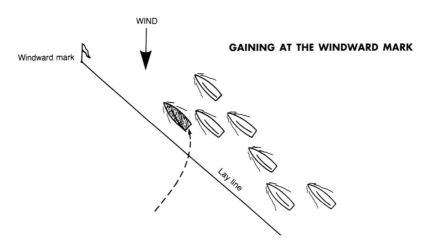

GAINING AT THE WINDWARD MARK

Top: Sailing the favored side of the upwind leg: on up-wind legs, the fleet will usually split—half will go to the right side of the weather leg and half will go to the left. In most cases one of the groups will come out ahead due to changes in wind direction. Some racers stay in the middle of the course until they detect which side of the course is favored. Here, as the wind shifts left, the boats on the left are initially headed on starboard tack. When they tack over, however, they are lifted up to the mark inside the boats to the right side of the course. The left side of the course is the favored side of the course. As soon as boat A discovers that the left side of the course is favored, it can tack over and reap the benefits. **Bottom:** Gaining at the windward mark: all the boats approaching the mark on starboard tack are overstanding the windward mark by sailing a course to windward of the lay line. They are all sailing extra, unnecessary distance. If you approach the mark on port tack (dotted line) and tack right on the lay line, you can pick up a couple of places.

Top: A crowd at the mark: in situations like these, make sure you know your racing rules and strive for a position with the clearest air possible. Note the roll tack of the skipper on the boat rounding the mark, and the skipper's far-forward position on the boat still running. **Left:** Overtaking to windward: you can work your way to windward over your opponents if you diligently concentrate on keeping your boat speed up, responding immediately to wind shifts, and sailing the boat flat. As soon as your opponent heels or fails to respond to a shift—assuming you keep your boat flat and play the wind shifts—you'll gain some distance and will eventually work your way past.

windward of his wake, you still have a chance. The idea is to wait for the other skipper to make a mistake—generally in the form of misjudging a shift or incorrectly handling a puff or lull. Keep your boat as flat as possible and continually up to speed. Figure that each time the other boat fails to respond to a shift immediately and you do, you have gained. Also, each time the other boat heels and you remain flat, you gain; heeling not only slows the boat, but causes it to sideslip as well. Eventually, you will grind over the top of your opponent." If you can sail the rest of the weather leg with equal persistence, you will inevitably end up near the top by the time you reach the weather mark.

Weather Mark Roundings

Weather marks tend to demand the greatest amount of mark-rounding skill. In the majority of Laser races, unless you are clearly first or last, you will likely be rounding in the company of a large number of other boats. The most important advice one can follow when sailing with so many other boats is to be thoroughly familiar with the rules regarding mark roundings. If in doubt, consult the ISAF or US SAILING rule books and their respective appeals.

Assuming you have a working knowledge of the rules, the next objective is to make a proper approach to the weather mark. There are a number of strategies to use, depending on each mark-rounding situation. If you are among the leaders, your main goal in rounding should be to break away from the fleet as quickly as possible after the rounding. The best method of doing this, assuming you are sailing a standard Laser course where marks are rounded to port, is to come into the mark on starboard tack. Starboard tack boats will have better boat speed when rounding because they will not have to perform a tack just before rounding. With a starboard tack approach, you can come into the mark with speed and momentum and immediately pop up on a plane, assuming there is enough wind. If you are making your approach on port tack, you will sacrifice momentum and speed as you tack around the mark. As a result, you will not be able to get the boat planing as quickly.

In certain situations, a port tack approach to the weather mark can work to your advantage. If the line of starboard tack boats is well spread out and you can see some spaces in the line, you can approach on port tack and find yourself a good position in the starboard tack lay line. This tactic

is especially good if you are back in the fleet. But be certain that there are some openings in the line, and make your approach a reasonable distance from the mark to allow room to either cross some bows or duck some sterns. Remember, Lasers tend to sideslip much more when in disturbed air and water. So it is better to sail a little beyond the lay line; you can then definitely lay the mark rather than risk extra tacks to fetch it.

Stewart Neff points out another advantage of a port tack approach: "Many times, unless you are right up with the top sailors, boats will not be hitting the lay lines correctly—they often badly overstand them. By coming in on port and tacking underneath them, you can often pick up a number of places. There are times when this can be risky, such as when boats are closing in on the mark in fairly tight formation." Remember that the current rules restrict a boat coming in on port tack within two boat lengths from the mark.

If it does appear that there will be a large group coming into the weather mark at one time, there is a solution recommended by Ed Adams, who has probably participated in more major Laser championships than anyone, and in the process has won the U.S. Midwinters and Nationals, British Nationals, two British Airways Opens, and was third at the 1976 Worlds. "I like to work above the starboard tack lay line and reach in over the top of the pack. Since most of them will be moving slowly, as they are likely pinching to round the mark, it is easy to pick up a number of places. Taking the outside route also reduces the chances of bumping another boat, which besides often stopping you dead in the water can also get you disqualified. You are also much less likely to end up pinned in someone else's wind shadow on the next leg with this tactic. And, because of the speed with which you round the mark, you will initially have a substantial speed advantage, especially if the next leg is a reach."

Occasionally, you may find yourself short of the lay line, but in a position that does not quite merit two extra tacks to fetch the mark. In this case, says Menkart, "Just keep your speed up by sailing normally, and don't try to pinch. The

Laser goes much slower and sideslips much more when pinching. You may not be pointing quite as high as if you were pinching, but you will actually end up in about the same spot, and you'll get there more quickly. If necessary, luff up sharply right as you get to the mark to pull yourself around it."

Once you have reached the weather mark, you must make an efficient rounding. Steer the boat around the mark with your weight by heeling the boat to windward. At the same time, ease the mainsheet gradually, but not quite as far as you might initially expect because the sudden heeling to windward keeps the apparent wind well forward. As you round, you should feel the boat accelerate and you should have minimal pressure on the tiller. Top Laser sailors can round marks without even moving the tiller, which means there is virtually no drag being created by the rudder. Once the turn is completed, the apparent wind will shift aft and the mainsheet may be eased for that leg of the race.

Offwind

The main goals of offwind sailing—whether reaching or running—are to keep your air clear, to maintain speed, and to work into a position that will leave you on the inside at the next mark rounding. In a big fleet, to be leeward of a group of boats or on the outside of a jammed-up rounding will only cost you positions; try to avoid those situations.

On the first reach, your route to the reach mark is largely dictated by your position in the fleet and the steadiness of the wind. If you have a good position, you can usually head straight for the mark. To maintain maximum boat speed, sail up in the lulls and down in the puffs. If there is a big group of boats directly behind, however, you will probably have to work upwind slightly to prevent them from riding to weather of you and taking your wind. Don't work up too high, though, for you will eventually have to sail back down to the reach mark on a more downwind course; that point of sail will be considerably slower.

In puffy conditions or in a wind that is building, it is best to sail high of the rhumb line. By being to windward of the other boats, you will be first to receive the new wind each time it fills in. Since the Laser is much like any other planing dinghy in that it is very responsive to slight increases in wind velocity, great speed gains can be made by following this strategy.

If there is a group of boats just ahead of you, many places can be gained by sailing lower than

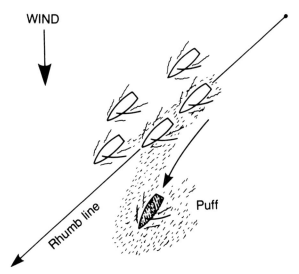

WIND

Rhumb line

Puff

Sailing below the rhumb line in a dying breeze: on the first reach, if the wind dies and puffs become fewer, drive down with them. Stay in each puff as long as you can. Sailing low allows you to come into the next mark on a closer reaching angle, meaning you'll be going faster than had you remained high. Plus, you'll be on the inside at the mark rounding.

the rhumb line. This is especially effective if the wind is steady or dying and you can keep your air clear. If you are low of the rest of the fleet and the wind begins to die, you will be able to continue a bit longer than those to windward, thus improving your position. Once you reach the point where you have to head up to fetch the mark, you will be sailing at a much improved angle to the wind and will have better boat speed than those who stayed on the rhumb line or went high. In addition, you'll be in an advantageous inside position at the reach mark rounding, assuming it is to be rounded to port.

The second reach of a Laser course can be sailed much the same as the first, except that now the advantages of going high have doubled. Not only will you have clearer air by going high, but you will also stay on the inside in preparation for the leeward mark rounding. Like the first reach, the main caution is not to go so high that you will eventually have to come down to a slower broad reach to fetch the leeward or reach mark.

One technique that allows you to get by a group of boats on the reaches is to move into what is known as "the passing lane." The theory is that large groups of boats sailing along on a reach have a snow-fence-like effect on the wind, forcing it to rise just before it reaches them and pass over the tops of their sails. Generally the wind starts lifting three or four mast heights to windward of them. Thus, all boats in the *fence* end up going slower than normal. If you are behind such a group, head up much higher than usual and sail a reaching course parallel to the fence, but far enough to windward so you will not be affected by this lifting pattern of the wind; in Lasers, this amounts to about 15 to 25 yards. The result is that you will be much faster and be gaining positions, even if you do have to sacrifice a few places when you eventually sail back down to the mark.

On runs, there is no substitute for sheer boat speed. Keep your air clear and watch the wind behind you so you can always be in the puffs rather than the lulls. Also keep on the favored jibe; if the wind is slightly to your left as you sail the rhumb line to the mark, then sail it on port tack. If it is to the right, sail it on starboard. To determine where the wind is, watch

Mark rounding: port tack Laser 8372 would be smart to go slow and try to sneak inside Laser O's transom to windward. Following the path of the two leading Lasers and ending up to leeward of them would work to 8372's disadvantage; it would end up in bad air and would sail a longer course than the leaders to windward. If 8372 could sneak inside O's transom but could not work its way to windward over O, at least 8372 would have the option to tack away for clear air.

your telltales or masthead fly, and keep an eye on the sail's leech. If you start sailing by the lee, the leech will begin to fold in toward the center of the windward side of the sail. Watch your speed relative to surrounding boats. You may discover occasions when sailing by the lee is very fast. This is covered in more detail in chapters 6 and 11. Finally, try to work your boat into an inside position in preparation for the leeward mark rounding.

Buzz Reynolds offered a few specifics about what to do should you end up directly behind someone on an offwind leg. "If the other sailor is slower than you, try to work up to windward of your opponent. Don't get right on their stern and then try to pass or, as the give-way boat, you may be forced to sail high and lose distance. Instead, stay a few boat lengths above them, to convince them that chasing upwind to head you up isn't worth it. If your opponent is faster, do all you can to stay with him. The best way to do that is get in his leeward wake and try to ride it as long as possible. That, plus steering and sheeting the sail to take best advantage of the waves, should allow you to hang in there."

Leeward Mark Roundings

One of the most difficult aspects of a leeward mark rounding is getting around the mark quickly without losing any ground to leeward on your new upwind heading. You must not only trim in a lot of sheet, but must also have complete control of the helm so you can steer smoothly around the mark. To do this, trim the mainsheet with both hands, across your body, while hanging on to the tiller with just a couple of fingers of your aft hand. Assuming a port rounding, sheet in with your left hand by pulling the line across your chest and placing it between the thumb and forefinger of your right hand (the rest of your fingers on your right hand will be holding the tiller extension). Hold the sheet in your right hand and repeat the process, using full arm extensions of your left hand to pull in the maximum amount of sheet each time you trim. Drop the excess line in the cockpit.

An even faster technique is hand over hand sheeting. Place your left hand on the sheet where it exits the cockpit block. Rapidly extend your left arm straight up, or across your aft shoulder, a full arm's length. With your right hand, while holding the end of the tiller extension and steering, grab the sheet as it exits the cockpit block, and in turn raise it straight up (in an arc, the length of the tiller extension). Rapidly bring your left hand back to the cockpit block, grab the sheet and bring in several more feet by pumping your arm up again. Repeat the process with your hand at the end of the tiller extension, and so on, until all the sheet is in. The ideal length of the tiller extension for this technique is 44 inches or a total of 81 inches measured from the base end of the tiller to the end of the tiller extension when fully extended forward.

In either case, as you trim, you must also be steering. In light and medium winds, much of the steering can be done by heeling the boat slightly to leeward, which means you will not be slowing the boat by putting pressure on the helm. Assuming you have the room to round, the best leeward mark rounding is one that comes into the mark wide, then as you head up to a close-hauled course, you cut the mark closely. In a Laser, coming in wide usually means between one-half to one boat length from the mark. As you head up to your new course, the mark should pass within inches.

If you find yourself on the outside of three or more boats that are going to be rounding the leeward mark together (called a *pinwheel*), don't just stay in formation and let them keep you on the outside. Not only will you be going slowly because of the disturbed wind and water, but you'll also be sailing a weather leg that is much longer than the rest of the fleet. Instead, as you get within two or three boat lengths of the mark (the distance varies depending on the speed of the boats), slow down by trimming in your sail or

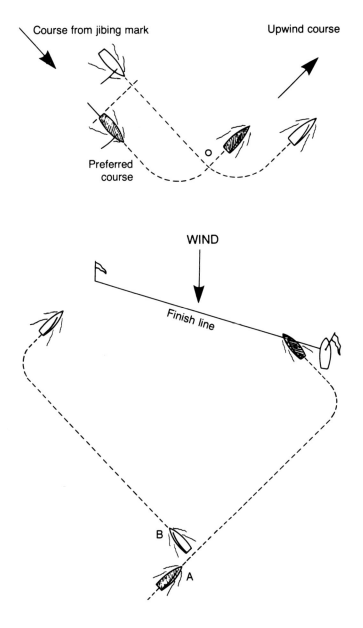

Course from jibing mark

Upwind course

Preferred course

WIND

Finish line

B

A

Top: A preferred mark rounding: when rounding a leeward mark before an upwind leg, concentrate on approaching the mark wide at first and then cutting it close as you round. This offers two advantages. First, it discourages anyone from trying to sneak in between you and the mark. Second, it puts you in the windward-most position on the upwind leg. **Bottom:** Favored end at the finish: boat A sees that the finish line is not square to the wind and heads for the leeward-most end of the line, which is the closest end of the line. A then beats B by sailing the shorter course. If the finish line was square to the wind, all points on the line would be the same distance from A and B's position. The courses that A and B would then sail would be equal in distance.

sailing a zigzag course, letting the other boats move a boat length ahead of you. Then, as they round the mark, head up sharply so you are right on the transom of the innermost boat, and round right behind or inside of it. You may be in that boat's bad air for a while, but you will have moved ahead of boats on the outside of the rounding, and you have also gained the option of tacking to clear your air or reach a more favorable side of the course.

Finishing

There are a few general rules for finishing that can often mean the difference of several places. First, finish at one end of the starting line or the other—it seldom pays to finish in the middle. Like midline sag at the start, competitors can have difficulty determining the exact location of the finish line. Delay making the final decision about which end to finish at for as long as possible. As you get closer to the line, your assessment of which end is favored will be more accurate. If you can preserve all of your options until the last moment, your chances of losing ground are considerably lessened.

If you are neck-and-neck with several other boats, generally the boat closest to the committee boat end will be hailed as having crossed the line first. The one exception to this is when the committee boat is very large and the person calling the line is well above the water. Then, because Laser hulls are so low to the water, it will be almost impossible to sight the bow of the boat finishing right next to the committee boat. What often happens is that the committee sights the masts on the boats nearest them and the hulls on boats further away. Be sure to cross the finish line of the tack that makes your course as perpendicular to the line as possible. This will save you considerable time and distance.

Race Course Guidelines

Before the Start

Know the course; get to the starting area 30 minutes ahead of time; practice tacks, jibes, and mark roundings. Take wind readings, determine tacking angles, set sail controls for the conditions, develop a starting plan.

The Start

Know the favored end, the length of the line (time to run it), the transit (range/line sight), the current (if any). Start at full speed on the line with clear air (make and protect hole to leeward, squeeze boat to weather).

The Beat

Have and follow your plan, but pick lanes with clear air; stay with the fleet (avoid fliers); cross the fleet when you can, don't let them cross you; observe the sailing angles (concentrate on sailing the closest tack to the mark); in light air, don't tack without a good reason; go for the wind (not the shift); foot by sheeting out if necessary; tack short of the layline unless close to the mark.

Downwind

Concentrate on speed and waves; balance boat to keep helm neutral; stay between the competitors and the mark (small fleet); avoid the middle (large fleet); check and hail for any overlaps; avoid a pinwheel (slow down and round on inside) at the mark; round the mark outside-in (enter wide, exit close).

The Finish

Stay on closest tack to finish and/or cover closest competitor; finish at the favored end and on the favored tack (if in doubt, tack for the downwind layline first); in a close situation, plan to finish on starboard tack. Put your best effort here, because everyone else is tired.

FIVE

Advanced Techniques Upwind

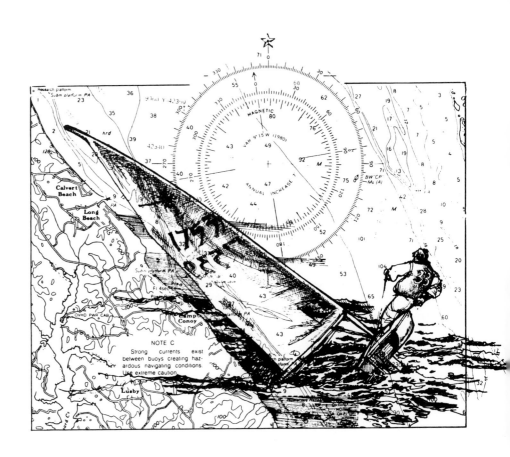

Those who watched John Bertrand win the 1977 Laser Worlds in Brazil quickly noted that, in large part, his success was due to his ability to sail the boat 100 percent all the way around the course, particularly upwind. When he passed boats late in the race, it was not because his speed had increased; others had simply tired and slowed down.

Bertrand's upwind ability, however, amounted to more than just top physical conditioning. He had also developed excellent upwind technique. Obviously, not everyone has as much time or energy to devote to training as Bertrand, but there are a number of upwind techniques that can optimize your performance. The basis of these techniques is suggested by one of the best natural racers in the U.S., Seattle sailor Carl Buchan. Buchan came close to winning the 1976 Worlds in Kiel, Germany, and won the U.S. Nationals twice. He sailed to his second Nationals win in a boat right off the racks of the University of Washington sailing club, demonstrating that it doesn't take a "super boat" to win a major Laser championship.

"I follow three basic rules for upwind sailing," says Buchan. "First, I always try to keep the boat as flat as possible. Second, I sheet the main just a bit tighter than I think I should. Third, I think of my body, the mainsheet, and the tiller as integral parts of the boat. Whenever the boat's course or angle of heel changes, all of those must be moved or adjusted accordingly." With Buchan's rules in mind, let's consider the three main types of sailing conditions you will encounter.

Light Air (0 to 8 knots)

Generally, when the wind is light, the water is smooth. The result is that you can usually sit much further forward in the boat than in any other wind condition. That gets the stern out of the water, allowing a smooth flow off the aft sections of the boat, and it helps neutralize the helm. In extremely light air, many racers sit ahead of the centerboard with their weight situated to allow the boat to heel to leeward 5 to 10 degrees; this is the only exception to the upwind rule about sailing the boat flat. The slight heel helps reduce wetted surface, allowing the boat to move through the water with less resistance. Most sit right on the centerline with their feet to leeward. In such light air, the amount the boat sideslips because of the heel is practically negligible. As the wind builds in the light air range, slowly begin moving your weight aft to the very front edge of the cockpit and start sailing the boat flatter. You can even try heeling the boat to weather, which sometimes allows you to gain height, or gauge.

One particularly successful light air sailor is Stewart Neff. At 195 pounds, he was one of the class heavyweights; yet, he won the 1979 U.S. Nationals, which was sailed entirely in light air. "The key to light air sail trim," says Neff, "is proper sheet tension. Think of the mainsheet as a draft control. The tighter you pull it, the more the mast will bend and the flatter the sail becomes. As you ease it, the spar straightens and creates a fuller sail. So that the amount of fullness I can carry is not restricted, I carry virtually no vang when the wind is under five knots. However, unless I'm suddenly in some rough chop, such as powerboat waves, where I need a lot of power, I almost always have enough tension on the sheet to bend the mast two or three inches."

When adjusting the mainsheet tension in light air (actually, when adjusting the draft), do so very slowly and easily, avoiding any sudden sheet movements. As a small puff hits, let the boat accelerate, then sheet in slightly to flatten the sail a bit. That helps bring the boat up to top speed. As the puff passes, ease the sheet to make the sail fuller, providing the power to keep moving.

The cunningham is generally not tensioned in light air, especially in winds under five knots.

Sitting forward in light air: in extremely light air, many Laser sailors sit very far forward—sometimes even ahead of the centerboard—and allow the boat to heel 5 to 10 degrees to leeward. This is the only wind condition in which you want to heel the boat upwind. Sailing with a leeward heel and with the stern slightly out of the water reduces wetted surface and allows the boat to move through the water with less resistance.

Once the wind increases a bit more than that, begin applying just enough cunningham tension to remove the wrinkles along the luff. Some racers have discovered the value of sailing with a loose cunningham, even up into medium air. One of those is Ed Baird, who won the 1980 Worlds in Kingston, Ontario, and two consecutive U.S. Midwinter championships: "I found that sailing with a loose cunningham, even to the point of having a lot of wrinkles along the sail luff, allows me to point high while maintaining good speed. I carry it loose until I can no longer hold the boat perfectly flat. Then I begin tightening it until the boat becomes level again. The theory behind the loose cunningham is that it creates a tight leech and moves the draft further aft. That also sharpens the angle of attack. Both of those are major factors in upwind performance."

Unless your outhaul is rigged with an 8:1 purchase as described in chapter 11, Dave Olson's Interview, it is fairly difficult to adjust while sailing, and any sudden movements in light air can quickly destroy momentum. Thus, most sailors set the outhaul once for light air upwind legs and leave it. The foot of the sail, at the point of maximum draft, should be about 4 inches off the boom in smooth water and 6 inches off in chop. The main traveler should be just snug, with the traveler block as far to leeward as possible.

In drifting conditions, you may have to carry the boom as far out as a foot or so beyond the leeward transom corner. Have just enough vang tension to bend the mast about 2 inches, which will flatten the sail somewhat. If your sail is too full, the light air will have difficulty traveling around that large a curve, will separate from the sail, and power will be lost. If the sail is a bit flatter, the air can move around the curved surface much more easily, allowing the flow to remain attached and thus preserving power.

Avoid unnecessary tiller movements. Instead, use your weight to steer: allow the boat to heel a few degrees more to leeward when you want to head up, and flatten the boat, or even heel it to windward a few degrees, to make it bear off. Don't try to point too high, as the boat will

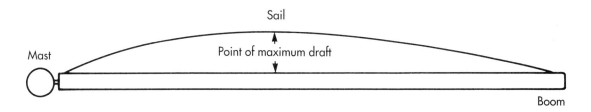

Controlling sail draft: maximum draft is the point where the sail is furthest from the boom. This distance should be about 4 inches in smooth water. In choppy water, where you need a fuller sail for more power to drive through the waves, this distance should be about 6 inches. You control the draft by tightening or easing the outhaul.

quickly stall out. You may not be pointing as high as those pinching and sheeting tighter, but you'll be more than making up that lost distance by going faster. Finally, move as carefully as you can, for each movement can drastically change the attitude of the hull to the water and the sail to the breeze.

Medium Air (8 to 16 knots)

The cardinal rules for medium air are to keep the boat flat all the time, set the sail up for as much power as you can possibly handle, and keep tiller movements to an absolute minimum. Let's take these ideas one at a time.

The best method of keeping the boat flat is to simply hike as hard as possible (assuming that you have not set the rig up for too much power). This is where sheer strength and endurance come into play. In medium winds, even lightweight sailors can keep up with their heavier competitors if they are hiking well.

A hiking method that has become popular among all of the top Laser sailors is straight-leg hiking. Its advantages are that it moves your weight further outboard than traditional bent-leg hiking and keeps your posterior from dragging in the water, which slows the boat. As the name implies, straight-leg hiking requires holding your legs very straight. To do this, it is important to have the length of your hiking strap set properly. When you are correctly positioned, your legs

should be virtually parallel to the water; you should feel equal pressure on both your calves and thighs.

Once in the straight-leg hiking position, you can respond to wind velocity changes by simply swinging your upper body in or out, as necessary. This is much smoother and more effective than the "all-or-nothing" bent-leg hiking technique. Straight-leg hiking does require conditioning and a lot of strength, particularly in the thigh muscles. Once mastered, though, the speed gained will be well worth the effort.

When setting up the sail for medium air, strive for as much power as possible. If you find you cannot hold the boat flat, depower by flattening the sail. If you find you're not fully hiked out and the wind is near the upper end of the medium range, make the sail fuller.

The main power adjustments are the outhaul, cunningham, and vang. The mainsheet is now used primarily to position the boom horizontally, unlike the vertical tension it controls in lighter air; use the vang to hold the boom down. To properly set the vang, get the main traveler as tight as possible and trim the mainsheet until the block on the end of the boom is right up against the traveler block. This is known as *two-blocking*. When the mainsheet is two-blocked, pull the slack out of the vang. With the mainsheet used to move the boom inboard and outboard and the vang to hold the boom down, the outhaul and cunningham can be adjusted to make the sail fuller or flatter. If you reach the point where the cunningham and outhaul are as tight as possible—and are therefore reducing the power of the sail—and you still can't hold the boat flat, tighten the vang further. By the same token, if the cunningham and outhaul are quite loose, and you feel you are not generating enough power, loosen the vang slightly.

Keeping tiller movements minimal in medium winds means steering the boat almost entirely with your weight and sail trim. Carl Buchan uses a method of turning the boat called *torquing*. Says Buchan, "This technique involves actually twisting the boat around with your body. To bear off, start in a fully hiked position [preferably a straight-leg position] with the boat flat. In

one smooth, deliberate movement, swing your upper body forward and twist your aft shoulder outboard. The pressure on your aft foot in the hiking strap should increase, while that on your forward foot should decrease. The torque you create will force the bow to leeward and the boat will bear off. To head up, reverse the movement—swing your upper body aft and twist your forward shoulder outboard. This time, you should feel more pressure on your forward foot in the hiking strap, and the bow will move to windward, heading up the boat."

Torquing by itself is good for minor course alterations in medium air, but if you must bear off more than a few degrees, such as when dropping below the stern of a boat on starboard tack,

Hiking styles: straight-leg (1) versus bent-leg (2) hiking. Straight-leg hiking moves your weight further outboard than bent-leg hiking and helps keep your posterior out of the water. When you are straight-leg hiking properly, your legs will be about parallel to the water and you will feel equal pressure on your calves and thighs.

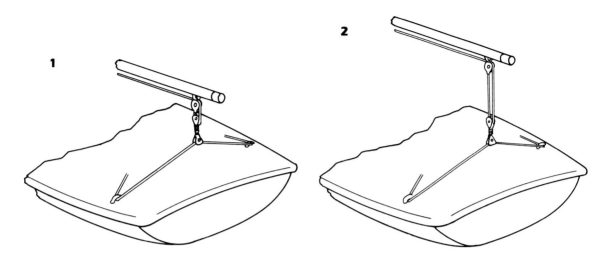

Two-blocking the main: **(1)** mainsheet that is two-blocked. The traveler should be as tight as possible. **(2)** The mainsheet prior to two-blocking.

How the leech affects pointing: Ed Adams (10699) demonstrates how a tight leech can improve pointing ability. Adams' outhaul, traveler, and mainsheet are trimmed much tighter, which all help tighten the leech. Notice the difference between the two leeches and how that enables Adams to point so much higher than his opponent.

more than torquing is necessary. One sailor with excellent boat handling technique is Andrew Menkart. "To bear off," says Menkart, "I always ease the mainsheet slightly to keep from getting overpowered when sailing slightly off a close-hauled course. The eased mainsheet also keeps the boat from heeling and helps maintain a neutral helm. I also slide aft 5 or 6 inches whenever I have to bear off substantially. That keeps the bow from digging in, which can prevent the boat from turning efficiently."

A large course alteration to leeward not only requires torquing and easing the mainsheet, but actually heeling the boat 5 to 10 degrees to windward in the process. To head up again after bearing off, simply sheet in and torque the boat slightly. In medium winds, heeling the boat to leeward to get it to head up is inefficient and generally ends up costing distance to windward because of sideslipping. To determine whether you are heading up and bearing off properly, note how much pressure you feel on the tiller during those maneuvers. If there is any more pressure than when sailing a straight course, you are sacrificing speed by using the rudder as a brake.

Heavy Air (16 knots and above)

In heavy air, the sailor who comes closest to holding his boat completely flat for the longest amount of time will generally be among the fastest. Often, this is determined by skipper size, but good technique can often allow light sailors to keep up with the heavies in a blow.

Regardless of the technique, top speed and pointing ability cannot be attained unless the sail is properly set. The most important heavy air adjustment is the vang, because it helps maintain sail shape by preventing the mast from straightening, even when the mainsheet is eased. (See Upwind Sail Adjustments chart, page 25.) Both light and heavy sailors should carry the vang as tight as possible. The easiest way to accomplish this is with a 6:1 vang. However, if you do not have the extra purchase provided by a 6:1 vang, you can use a technique developed years ago. First, tighten the main traveler and two-block the mainsheet. Now, put your aft hand on top of the boom, just ahead of where the forward mainsheet block is attached. Push down hard on the boom

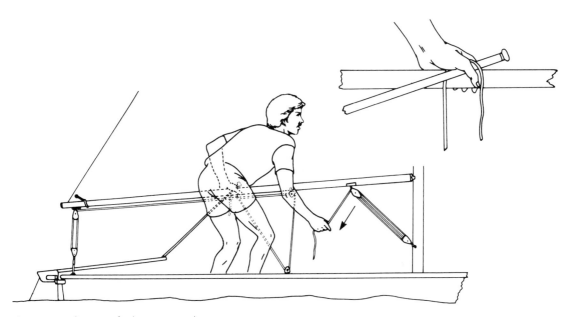

Super vang the main for heavy air sailing: see text.

with that hand and the mainsheet should go slightly slack. As that happens, take up the slack in the vang with your forward hand. The vang should now be tight enough to function as a *traveler*, and the mainsheet can be used just to move the sail in and out, as necessary, without causing the mast to straighten and the sail to become fuller. This is especially important in gusty conditions, when the last thing you want to do is make the mainsail fuller when you have to dump the sheet in a puff.

There is an alternative method of *super vanging* that can be done while sitting in the normal upwind position. The mainsheet must be two-blocked and firmly cleated for this technique. Place your forward foot on the mainsheet, either on the section of sheet running from the forward-most mainsheet block on the boom down to the mainsheet block just forward of the cockpit, or on the section of sheet just aft of the forward-most mainsheet block on the boom. By pushing hard in either place, you prebend the boom, thereby putting slack in the vang. While still pushing with your foot, reach over and simply pull the slack out of the vang. You now are super vanged and ready for great speed upwind.

Top: Super vanging using stock vang with 3:1 purchase with the jamming block on the boom; first, while close-hauled, make certain that the mainsheet is two-blocked and securely cleated. (1) Use your aft foot as shown to apply pressure to the mainsheet to prebend the boom. (2) While pushing down with your foot, reach forward and pull the slack out of the vang. **Bottom:** Super vanging using vang with 6:1 purchase (see chapter 11) with the jamming block on the mast; first, while closehauled, make certain that the mainsheet is two-blocked and securely cleated. (1) Use your forward foot to prebend the boom by pushing hard on the mainsheet between the boom block and center-mounted cockpit block. (2) While pushing hard with your foot, pull the vang line "super" tight.

The very best way to control vang tension is described in chapter 11, Dave Olson's tips on Recent Advances in Rigging Techniques.

The cunningham should also be extremely tight, often to the point where the cunningham sail grommet is pulled right down to, or below, the top of the boom. As in medium air, the outhaul should be adjusted according to your ability to hold the boat flat. If there is a lot of chop and you are fairly heavy, ease the outhaul so that the sail is 1 to 2 inches off the boom. This creates a fuller, more powerful sail. If you can't hold the boat flat, trim the outhaul back in to depower the sail.

If you have made all of the proper sail adjustments, are hiking as hard as you can, and still can't hold the boat flat, try raising the centerboard anywhere from 4 to 8 inches. This allows the boat to pass through the waves easier, significantly reducing some of the lateral resistance that contributes to a heeling moment.

Ed Baird suggests, "Another method of keeping the boat flat is to have the board all the way down, but, with an extremely tight vang, sheet out as necessary to hold the boat flat. The sail luff may not be full, but the leech will be, and because you are sheeted out so far, the force coming off the leech is more forward than sideways." That technique has allowed Baird, at 165 pounds, to keep up with much heavier sailors on very breezy windward legs.

Since heavy winds and heavy seas usually go hand in hand, fast upwind technique requires being able to sail effectively through waves. The best method is to steer an S-shaped course through them by alternately heading up into the crests and bearing off as the crests pass under the boat, all the while keeping the boat flat. There are several methods of doing this.

One method was suggested by Dave Perry, who was a top finisher at the 1979 Worlds in Australia: "I like to use very vigorous tiller movements. At times it may seem like you are slowing the boat by doing so, but it actually helps keep it flat. In the long run, you'll find yourself moving out to windward of those who allow their boats to heel and get knocked around by the waves."

Another method is used by Carl Buchan: "I torque the boat through the waves, using the body movements to force it to head up or bear off, coupled with slight tiller movements." This is especially effective for sailors at the heavier end of the scale, for their added weight makes torquing through the waves over long beats much easier. "When weaving through the waves by torquing," adds Buchan, "timing is extremely critical. Remember, the Laser will not begin heading up or bearing off at the exact moment you start the torque. Instead, it begins turning a moment or so later, so you must take that into account."

Finally, Buzz Reynolds uses a combination of Perry's and Buchan's techniques: "I make vigorous and continuous tiller movements, but each movement is accompanied by the appropriate torque. As the tiller is pulled to windward, my body torques forward, and I twist my aft shoulder outboard. In addition to that movement, I also lean my upper body inboard or outboard to keep the boat flat, depending on how strongly the gusts are coming through."

Roll Tacking

One technique all top Laser sailors use, without exception, is roll tacking. It is most effective in light and medium winds, although some top sailors can even employ it in heavy winds. A good roll tack creates increased lift during tacking, resulting in a smoother, faster tack that actually accelerates the boat through the maneuver rather than slowing it.

To learn to roll tack the Laser, try it when the winds are less than 6 to 8 knots. Begin with the boat close-hauled, up to speed, and perfectly flat. To initiate the roll tack, lean in to induce a slight leeward heel, then push the helm gently to leeward. As the boat begins to turn into the wind, hike out hard, heeling the boat to windward, but be sure to hold on to the tiller extension (a longer tiller extension makes this much easier). When hiking out, also slide aft 10 to 14 inches to lift the bow out of the water and allow the boat to pivot on its flatter, aft sections. If you don't slide aft, heeling the boat to windward may actually cause the boat to bear off, making an efficient tack impossible. At no time during the roll tack should you be facing aft. As you cross the cockpit, ease the sheet 3 to 4 feet (more in light air, less in heavier air) and exchange the tiller extension and mainsheet behind your back (see chapter 2, Tacking). As you reach the other side of the cockpit, get your feet under the hiking strap as quickly as possible and hike hard to pull the boat flat again, retrimming the mainsheet in the process. If you have made a good roll tack, the sail will not luff during the tack, but rather will *pop* from one tack to the other. You should also be able to feel the boat pick up speed during the tack, particularly in light air.

As the wind and waves build, roll tacking requires a little more speed and technique. Instead of just sliding aft 10 to 14 inches, you may have to slide back even more. This keeps the bow from digging into the waves and further helps torque the boat around.

An additional heavy air technique is used by Ed Adams: "I start the tack by hiking out only on my forward foot. Just before tacking, I place my aft foot on top of the hiking strap. Then, when I cross the cockpit, the heel of my aft foot touches down first, right next to the hiking strap. As I pivot my body around to the new windward side, turning on the heel of that foot, the toes of that foot automatically swing under the hiking strap. That allows me to get hiked out immediately, thus completing the tack more quickly. Once hiked out on the pivoting foot, I then slide my other foot under the hiking strap."

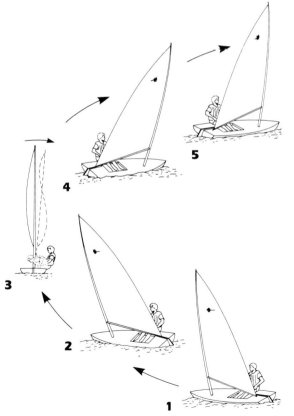

Roll tack: (1) Sailing flat. (2) Let the boat heel. (3) Hike to windward as you turn through the eye of the wind. (4) Bring it back up while sheeting in. (5) Hike it flat again.

SIX

Advanced Techniques Offwind

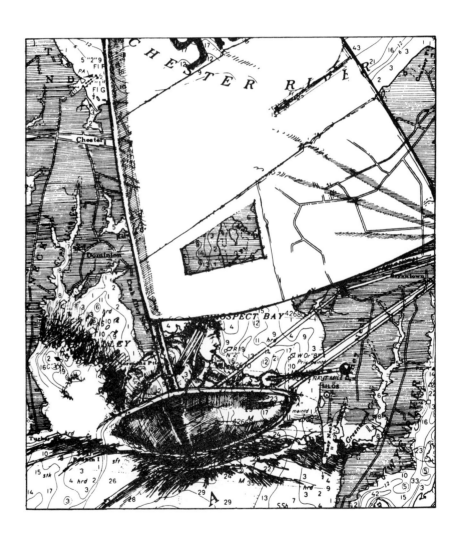

Offwind sailing can be the most exhilarating point of sail in a Laser, and can present prime opportunities for either increasing a lead or catching up. The difference in speed between a good and a fair Laser sailor can mean a lot of distance, and technique can often be more important than weight. Heavier class sailors, such as Carl Buchan (185 pounds) and Steward Neff (195 pounds), have won major light air championships; this dispells the notion that to do well, particularly offwind in light air, you must be a lightweight.

Before continuing, it is important to understand what you can and cannot do when sailing offwind, according to the current International Sailing Federation (ISAF) edition of the racing rules. When you encounter a wave large enough to surf, or if the wind velocity suddenly increases to where you can plane, you may give the mainsail one quick pump (rapidly trimming and releasing it). You may not continue pumping the sail until another wave comes along or the wind increases again. Also, you are not permitted to adjust your body, the sails, or the centerboard so that your boat begins persistently rocking (rolling from side to side). Finally, you may not *ooch*, or suddenly throw your body forward and then abruptly stop.

The idea behind these rules is to require a boat to compete by using only the wind and water to increase, maintain, or decrease her speed. If you are protested for violating the rules, you will have to prove that planing or surfing conditions

On a reach in a Radial Laser in medium winds, this skipper shows good form. She is holding the end of the tiller extension, palm down. Her hands are close together, facilitating hand-to-hand sheeting technique. The outhaul, cunningham, and 6:1 vang are all eased. The centerboard is halfway up and she is hiking enough to balance the boat with the helm in a neutral position.

existed and that you did not go beyond the prescribed limits for initiating planing or surfing by pumping. Rocking is still prohibited at all times. In drifting conditions, rocking a Laser will push it through the water at a surprising rate. It will help you get home on a windless day, but you may never rock during a race. With these rules in mind, let's examine the two types of offwind legs—reaching and running.

Reaching

The most important goal when going from a beat to a reach is to get the boat moving as fast as possible, as quickly as possible. Once you get the boat up to speed, then you can worry about fine-tuning adjustments, such as loosening the outhaul and cunningham. To get the boat up to top speed right away, play the main directly from the boom: this allows you to adjust sail position very quickly, keep the boat flat, and keep the helm as neutral as possible. To bear off, hike out harder to heel the boat to windward slightly, and ease the mainsheet a bit. To head up, slightly overtrim the main, which creates weather helm and turns the boat into the wind. Never allow the boat to heel to leeward on reaches, for all you will do is sideslip and sacrifice speed.

Once the boat is moving well, pull the centerboard up 18 inches or so, if you haven't already done this at or even before rounding the wind-

ward mark. Particularly on breezy reaches, it is better to carry the board a little higher than you might expect. John Bertrand and other top Laser sailors often carry their boards even higher on reaches than on runs. This is simply because they want to sail perfectly flat on reaches and are willing to sideslip a bit in return for it. In addition, because of the Laser's high speed on reaches, particularly when planing, and the boat's well-shaped centerboard, the board becomes very efficient on that point of sail; when the boat is sailed flat, very little board is actually needed to keep tracking.

Another important reaching adjustment—one that top Laser sailors have really focused on—is the vang. Especially in heavy winds, ease the vang an inch or two for the reach. This produces a fuller and more powerful sail shape, and prevents the boom from dragging in the water should you inadvertently end up heeling. The major problem is when and how to ease the vang.

Ed Baird says, "I make vang adjustment part of my weather mark rounding routine. As I am on the final approach to the weather mark, I am sheeted in tight. I then head up slightly, yet keep the boat flat. As that occurs, I reach forward and pop the vang line out of its cleat. Because the main is sheeted tight, there isn't that much tension on it, and it becomes fairly easy to do. To ensure the vang is not eased too much, I either

Broad reaching in heavy air: this skipper demonstrates good heavy air form. He is keeping the boat flat by straight-leg hiking. The centerboard is raised, and outhaul and cunningham are eased. The vang is tight enough to tension the leech properly without pulling the boom down so far that it will drag in the water should the boat heel slightly on a wave.

Driving over waves: to avoid losing speed by digging the bow into the back of a wave, Peter Commette slides way aft and gives the mainsheet a sharp tug to pop over a wave. Notice that he is straight-leg hiking to avoid slowing down by dragging his posterior in the water.

mark the line to provide a reference point or tie a figure-eight knot in the tail in a position that will preset vang tension for the upcoming reach. The advantage of this technique," says Baird, "is that while others are attempting to ease the vang after rounding the mark, you are automatically set up for reaching and can concentrate 100 percent on playing the waves and the wind. Plus, you will not lose that much ground when easing the vang upwind. Anyone close to windward will likely be forced up with you as you head up slightly; anyone to leeward will probably already be in your wind shadow."

For fine-tuning adjustments on reaches, Carl Buchan follows a couple of basic rules: "If I feel the boat is not picking up speed quickly enough in the puffs, I tighten the vang. If the boat feels like it is simply not moving well, or if I'm having trouble catching waves, I loosen the vang. I also ease the vang more in chop than in smooth water. In chop, I want a fuller sail with more twist. That also makes the sail more forgiving, preventing it from stalling as quickly as it might

if the sail was flatter and the leech tighter. In smooth water, there should be enough vang to hold the leech taut when a puff hits, forcing all power generated forward rather than spilling it off to leeward."

Vang adjustments are quite easy to make, using either the 6:1 purchase vang, or the optional block and tackle system.

Finally, ease the cunningham all the way on reaches. On wild, windy reaches this is not absolutely critical, for it is far more important to be out in the hiking straps, keeping the boat planing. But especially in light air, a loose cunningham makes the sail much fuller. Most sailors ease the outhaul on reaches, except in the lightest of conditions when the outhaul is usually already out for the preceding weather leg.

Weight placement on reaches depends largely on wind strength. The lighter the wind, the further forward you should be. In a drifter (0 to 3 knots), you should be almost up against the mast, yet not forward of it (which is prohibited by Laser class rules). In light air (3 to 8 knots), you should be at the forward end of the cockpit. In medium air (8 to 16 knots), position yourself in the middle of the cockpit. In heavy air (over 16 knots), you should be as far aft and out as possible.

As on other points of sail, always adjust your weight so that the helm stays neutral, which may entail heeling the boat slightly to windward in very light reaching conditions. If the helm is not aligned with the centerboard, the angled rudder creates extra drag in the water. This will slow you down tremendously.

In rough seas, you can make huge gains on the reaches by playing the waves. The idea is to work or steer the boat down or across the waves, much the same as a surfer coasts down the slope of a wave. When you are going slower than the waves, as often happens when reaching in light air, it is important to surf as many waves as possible and maintain each surf as long as you can. To catch a wave, you need to get up as much speed as possible, while trying not to use the rudder at all—steer with your weight. When you see a catchable wave approaching from behind, move your weight inboard; this will cause the boat to head up slightly and increase your speed. Then, as the wave begins to lift your stern, bear off sharply by suddenly hiking out, heeling the boat to windward and giving the main the legal one to three pumps to initiate the surf. Ed Adams suggests, "Place your forward-most foot against the front of the cockpit. When you are ready to bear off down a wave, lunge not only outboard, but aft, and give the mainsheet a good pump in the process. As you start riding the wave, carefully get the boat level again and move forward to keep the boat pointing down in the trough." When you catch a good wave, the feeling is sensational; you'll know when you've done it right.

In heavier air, when you are moving faster than the waves, it is critical to prevent the waves from slowing you down. The main cause of speed loss is digging the bow into the back of a wave. For this reason, keep your weight as far aft as possible. In addition, always try to keep the boat heading for the low spots in the waves—the troughs. If it appears you have no choice but to sail up the back of a big wave, head up slightly so that you will be able to sail a faster, traversing route, rather than a directly up-hill one. In such conditions, you should be continually adjusting the mainsheet as the apparent wind changes when your boat slows or speeds up. Top sailors can tell this simply by feel—the boat will slow and they'll automatically ease the mainsheet 4 to 6 inches as the apparent wind shifts aft and vice versa. But if you have trouble sensing that, keep an eye on your sail telltales, particularly ones on the sail luff. Always try to let the sail out; ease it until the windward telltale begins to luff, then trim slightly. If in doubt, it's much faster to have the sail out too far than overtrimmed. If you do end up trying to work up the back of a wave, do so at maximum speed. Then, once at the top of the wave, give the mainsheet a good tug to pull you over the top and start planing again.

Planing itself is not all that difficult, as it is something even first-time Laser sailors can get the boat to do on a breezy reach. The keys are to keep the boat flat by making sure the main is sheeted out far enough and, occasionally, giving the sheet a good pump to initiate the plane. Once planing, the board becomes very efficient and can be raised. The helm will also neutralize, and even the most subtle movement of the tiller will send the boat veering sharply to windward or leeward. In racing, what makes planing difficult is the ability to plane over long distances. Almost everyone will be planing at one time or another on the reaches, but the one who planes the longest will gain the most. The idea is to keep the boat traveling with the least resistance, and at the same time always try to sail in the areas of strongest wind. The difficulty is that those two places are not always the same, and for that reason, keeping a boat planing requires a lot of concentrating on the course ahead. Always keep the bow driving for the troughs and try to stay in the darker patches of water that usually indicate puffs. If the wind lightens, or you sail out of a puff, head up slightly. This increases your apparent wind and may keep you planing. When hit with a puff, drive off to leeward by heeling the boat to windward to regain any territory you lost in the lulls.

The key to reaching, whether in waves or planing conditions or not, is to sail with as little helm movement as possible. Let your body movements and sail trim control where the boat is heading—it's much faster.

Downwind in heavy air: this sailor opts for a reefed sail, which helps him to sail fast in perfect control. Notice that the clew is pulled as close to the boom as possible, the outhaul is drumtight, and, even though sailing downwind, the centerboard is almost completely down for added stability.

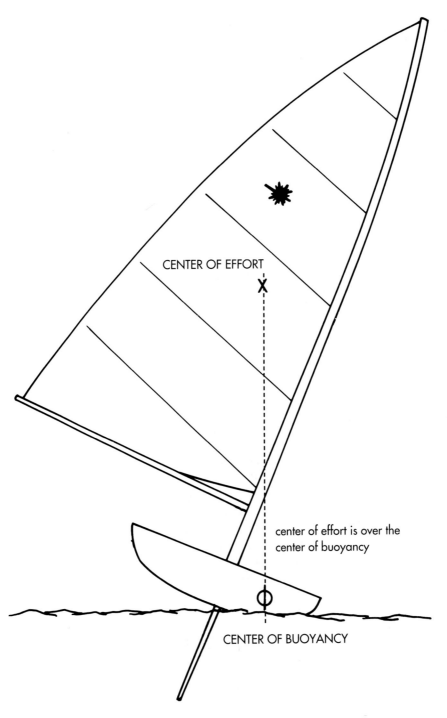

CENTER OF EFFORT

X

center of effort is over the
center of buoyancy

CENTER OF BUOYANCY

Heel to windward when running for better balance: a
windward heel helps bring the center of effort in line with
the center of buoyancy. The alignment of these two points
produces better boat balance and reduces weather helm.

Running

Running before the wind is the Laser's most demanding point of sail in terms of balance and concentration. If the wind is light, you must concentrate on catching each little puff and keeping the boat moving all the time. If the wind is heavy, you must not only think about speed but must also be concerned with keeping the boat upright by continually adjusting sail trim and positioning your weight. Generally, you will go fastest on runs when you are right on the brink of disaster.

For sail trim, the cunningham should be eased all the way, except in heavy air when it should be just tight enough to take the wrinkles out of the luff. If you are on the heavy side and the wind is light, ease the outhaul to make the sail fuller.

Many Laser sailors, such as Stewart Neff, do not loosen the vang on runs, even though they do so slightly on reaches. "The idea," says Neff,

Top: Running in a light breeze: These boats are heeled to windward to maintain neutral helm and reduce wetted surface. This is fast. **Bottom:** Running in a strong breeze: Carl Buchan pops his boat up onto a wave by giving a sharp tug on the mainsheet, which he trims directly from the boom. He sails with the centerboard most of the way down to provide stability in wavy and heavy air conditions.

"is that a tight vang, especially in heavy winds, exposes a little more sail to the wind; the resultant tight leech will not hurt you nearly as much on a run as it will on a reach." However, in light air, it is best to adjust your vang for the wind velocity, loosening it if the boat feels sluggish and tightening it if the boat lacks acceleration.

The board is generally carried lower on runs than on reaches because the Laser is not as stable dead downwind as it is on reaches. Carl Buchan suggests, "Sail with the board up as far as you dare, but if the boat starts oscillating too much, lower it some." Generally, Buchan simply carries the board halfway up in almost all downwind conditions. "Make sure there is always at least a few inches of board sticking out of the bottom of the boat," says Buchan. "The added turbulence of an open centerboard slot is not worth the reduced drag of a fully raised board." Also, if the board is raised too high, it can prevent the boom from crossing on a jibe, should you forget to lower it.

Pitchpole! Digging your bow into the back of a wave in high winds can have dramatic consequences. This Laser flipped with such force that the centerboard was driven out of the trunk. To avoid this, always try to keep your boat headed for the troughs in wavy waters. If you must sail up the back of a wave, head up slightly so that you sail a traversing—not a head-on—route over the wave.

Fore-and-aft body position when running is much the same as on reaches, with weight all the way forward in very light air and gradually moving aft as the wind velocity increases. For lateral balance, however, heel the boat slightly to windward, which helps align the sail's center of effort with the balance point of the hull. To a point, the more you heel to windward, the faster you'll go, but you will quickly discover that excessive windward heel makes the boat laterally unstable. Such instability in the form of violent rolling from side to side can result in a *death roll*, or capsize to windward. Death rolls occur most in heavy air, but if you have the sail out far enough, the board up a long way, and the boat heeled well to windward, a death roll can occur even in light air conditions. If you feel your boat starting to roll, begin by sailing it slightly more level. If that's not enough, lower the centerboard another 5 to 10 inches. If you're still rolling, trim the mainsheet 1 or 2 feet. In all but severe conditions, that should easily stabilize the boat. Another option is to work with the rolls, using them to help the boat accelerate. Whenever the boat starts to heel to windward, trim the mainsheet sharply. This applies force to leeward, halting the windward movement. Don't overdo this, as the rules prohibit making adjustments that make the boat continually oscillate. However, if you suddenly feel the boat taking a sharp lurch to windward, a quick trim on the main may well save you from taking an unwanted swim. One further method of dealing with death roll situations is to sail by the lee. It does, however, require some practice, as it involves positioning yourself on the leeward side of the boat, with the sail out a couple of feet beyond 90 degrees. But it does markedly improve stability and speed in heavy conditions by bringing the center of effort of the boat and sail more closely in line.

Like reaching, it is absolutely critical to sail runs with as little helm as possible. This means steering with your weight—heeling to leeward to head up and heeling to windward to bear off—and adjusting the mainsail with each change in wind or water conditions. So that you can tell whether you are getting any helm at all, Ed Adams recommends loosening the main traveler on runs. "That reduces friction between the traveler line and the top of the tiller," he says, "giving you a better feel for when the helm is neutral." But don't forget to tighten the traveler again before you round the leeward mark. Sailing in waves on the run is done the same way as on reaches—always keep the boat headed for the troughs and never try to drive up the back of a wave.

Roll Jibing

In a strong wind, a jibe can be a thrilling and safe maneuver, if done properly. The key to executing successful jibes, both run-to-run and reach-to-reach, lies in a combination of beginning the jibe when moving as fast as possible and making all of your movements very deliberate. Never attempt to jibe just as a puff hits; wait until you are well into the puff and at top speed. If you jibe then, there will be much less load on the rig, and your chances of capsizing will be much less. You'll discover the main jibes over smoothly, rather than slamming across.

For an efficient roll jibe, assume you are running on starboard tack and wish to jibe to port. You are sitting on the starboard edge of the cockpit, facing forward. First, make sure everything is set, particularly the board. If the board is up quite high and the wind is light, lower it a bit to provide more of a pivot point for the boat to turn on. If it is very windy, raise the board slightly; this allows the boat to skid as it goes over to the new jibe, rather than tripping over the board and capsizing.

Holding the mainsheet directly from the boom, hike out hard to roll the boat to windward. Generally, the lighter the wind, the further you can roll the boat over. In very light conditions, you may even put the windward rail underwater during the roll. The roll causes the boat to bear off, as you are using your weight to turn the boat rather than the rudder. As the leech starts to collapse, reach up and grab the mainsheet right ahead of the block on the boom and give it a sharp tug to start the boom across. As the boom crosses the cockpit, give the mainsheet another sharp tug; this kicks the slack out of the mainsheet and prevents it from snagging on the transom corner. Don't tug too hard, for it is possible to create enough of a whip in the mainsheet so that it becomes wrapped around the aft end of the boom. As the boom swings across, duck, slide to the other side of the boat, and hike hard to pull the boat level. However, don't hike so hard that you force the boat into another jibe. The idea is to hike just enough to pull the boat back to its normal angle of heel for those conditions. Particularly in light air, when you pull the boat back down from the jibe, you should feel the pressure on the mainsheet increase considerably, and the boat will accelerate.

Running for trouble: if you don't apply enough vang pressure when sailing downwind in heavy air, the upper half of the sail may lift to windward. This could help cause a *death roll*—a capsize to windward. More vang pressure would flatten the sail.

If you can do that while eliminating any pressure on the helm, you've probably just completed a good jibe. Once the jibe is over, take care of any adjustments you made before the jibe, such as changing the centerboard position.

For heavier sailors, or for anyone in light air, it often works well to jibe by facing aft, grabbing the two parts of the sheet near the transom, and rapidly swinging the sail across. In that case, you face the stern and remain near the center of the boat. Steer dead downwind or slightly by the lee as you reach for the sheets to pull the sail across. Although more difficult to do than in a roll tack, try to steer with your weight as much as possible. Once the leech starts folding in, give the sheets a solid tug, and the boat will jibe.

The art of sailing offwind smoothly and with speed and finesse comes only with practice. Almost anyone can sail the Laser offwind in light and medium air, but to handle it *well* in those and heavier wind conditions can only be learned through experience.

The art of sailing offwind smoothly and with speed and finesse comes only with practice.

SEVEN

Practice and Physical Fitness

Practice is necessary to maintain a certain degree of proficiency, regardless of one's sport. Because of the ever-improving caliber of Laser sailors, this is perhaps truer for the Laser than for some other one-design classes. Talk to any of the many past Laser champions—Ed Baird, John Bertrand, Carl Buchan, Andrew Menkart, Stewart Neff, Peter Commette, Ed Adams and more recently, Robert Scheidt, Ben Ainslie, Michael Blackburn, Nick Adamson—and you will discover a common denominator in their tactic for perfecting their skills: "time in the boat."

However, practice does not have to be drudgery, and for serious Laser sailors it can actually be fun and challenging. The most beneficial practice is to be had with one or a few other boats. This will provide good, head-to-head competition, particularly if those you are practicing with are as good as or better than you.

Boat against Boat

The most efficient way to develop speed is to sail alongside another Laser and attempt to match its speed. Get as close as possible without interfering with each other's wind; try to get side by side, one to two boat lengths apart. The skipper of the leeward boat becomes a "constant," sailing as fast as possible, but making no sail adjustments. The skipper of the windward boat makes changes in the various sail controls, one at a time, all the while carefully observing the effects on speed relative to the leeward boat.

Once the windward boat's skipper determines what changes have increased speed, the two skippers change roles—the "constant" now becomes the "experimenter" and vice versa. In this manner, each can quickly learn what makes the boat go fastest.

Informal Racing

The best way to get all-around practice is simply to race. We had a lot of fun doing this in Charleston, South Carolina, during the early years of the class. In the winter, a half dozen or so top Laser sailors gathered each Sunday for informal racing. We set up our own courses, using government buoys in the river, and either started ourselves or used a volunteer committee boat. If there are only two of you, a good way to practice is to set up a starting line, have one person give a two-minute preparatory signal and start. When one boat has clearly gained an advantage over the other, either by establishing a safe leeward position or by driving over the leeward boat, go back and start again.

With more than two boats, the two-minute starting sequence can still be effective and allows you to get in plenty of races. In Charleston, we started informally by establishing a line that was square to the wind, which was formed by a buoy at one end and a point of land at the other. The skippers were then on their own to make sure they were not over the imaginary line at the start. Other buoys in the river were used for the remaining marks of the course. If you do not have permanent marks in your racing area, it is fairly easy to construct portable marks using plastic Clorox bottles or milk containers, both of which can be easily seen on a short course.

Another method of increasing the competition is to line boats up, side by side, on the starting line according to how they did in each previous race. Reverse the order of finishers, positioning the first finisher in the least advantageous position, the second boat in the next position, and so on. This method works well for two to five boats.

For more than five boats, there is an informal start known as the *rabbit* or *gate start*, in which the wake of a boat on one tack is the starting line for all the other boats, all of whom are sailing on the other tack. The rabbit is the boat that sails across the fleet on port tack, hard on the wind. While the rabbit is making its run, it has complete right-of-way. The rest of the boats head to the line—the wake of the port tack boat—on starboard tack and duck the stern of the rabbit. After the entire fleet has passed behind the rabbit's stern, the rabbit may tack over to starboard. This requires a bit more skill than the other starts discussed, but for larger groups of boats, the rab-

The most efficient way to develop speed is to sail alongside another Laser and attempt to match its speed.

bit start is effective and fair; barring sudden wind shifts, it does not put anyone at a disadvantage.

The Slalom Course

An exciting diversion from the usual, round-the-triangle type of practice session is to sail a slalom course, either alone or, as in the San Francisco Laser Heavy Weather Slalom event, against someone else. Particularly in heavy air, it requires the skipper to tack and jibe at frequent intervals and gives boat handling ability a thorough test.

The slalom course consists of a number of buoys spaced equidistantly in a row that runs in line with the wind direction. Only the windward-most buoy is anchored; the rest are held in place by a weighted stringer line. The leeward-most buoy has a "sail" of sorts, which keeps the line of buoys running dead downwind, regardless of wind shifts. The object is to start at the leeward-most buoy and tack upwind between the buoys. After rounding the buoy farthest to windward, you then jibe downwind between the buoys. This rapid tacking and jibing required to sail the course is challenging and exciting, particularly under breezy, wavy conditions.

Competition can be introduced into the slalom by constructing two courses, side by side. Two boats can be given timed starts or started evenly from a dead luffing standstill. Whoever negotiates all of the buoys first wins. This is how the San Francisco Laser Heavy Weather Slalom was run. The event was scheduled for what was expected to be one of the windiest weekends of the year, which, of course, also meant big waves. Top sailors from across the country were invited to compete, tournament-style, on the double slalom course. The winner was the one who moved through the tournament bracket. Win or lose, sailing in any heavy weather slalom race is an unparalleled thrill.

Of course, there is no substitute for actual regatta experience, but a series of regular, well-structured practice sessions can help improve your Laser sailing tremendously. Every class champion has put in time on the water and then some. It's the only way to get there.

These sailors are practicing in racing gear and focusing on balance and sail controls.

Practicing Alone

Occasionally, you may not be able to practice with other boats. However, one can practice boat handling when sailing alone. Practice tacking, jibing, capsizing, and rounding marks. Develop smooth procedures and, through constant repetition, learn to execute all maneuvers without having to think about them. Eventually, you should begin feeling like a part of the boat. It will simply feel "right" when you execute maneuvers well, and it will be equally obvious when you have not.

Often, the windier it is, the more valuable practice time can be, particularly when practicing alone. In heavier wind conditions, boat handling skills can really be tested. Some time back, one of the top French Finn sailors was practicing on Switzerland's Lake Lucerne. The race committee had canceled the day's races because of strong, treacherous winds funneling between the steep mountains that surround the lake. But the Frenchman was out practicing, one jibe after another. Naturally, he turned over a few times, but he got more practice in those 15 minutes of heavy air sailing than many of the sailors who watched him from the shore got in one year. He loved every minute of it, too, because he knew he had an attentive shoreside audience.

Most top Laser sailors earn every trophy they win by spending hours practicing alone in their boats. An early example: Lasse Hjortnees, an 18-year-old Danish student, finished 39th at the 1978 Laser World Championship. Determined to win the 1979 Worlds, he sailed every day, except Christmas, from the end of the 1978 event to the beginning of the 1979 regatta. Hjortnees ended up topping the 93-boat fleet in 1979, giving him the title he had worked so hard for.

Physical Fitness

Nineteen eighty-two World Champion Terry Neilson, who also in 1980 won the Canadian and European Championships and the gold medal in the Pan American Games, often spent four hours a day on the water. Neilson says, "Everyone asks me what I do to go fast. People, even my good friends who sail with me all the time, still think there is some special secret I have that no one else knows. But that's not true. It's just being in good shape, concentrating, and a lot of practice."

To sail a Laser effectively, and especially to race successfully, you should be in good physical condition. Being in good shape is most important in upwind sailing when the boat must be kept flat and driven hard. You must give long-term, maximum effort under these conditions and should be in good enough shape so that the physical stress will not impair your concentration or your strategy and tactics.

On a short course, hiking is most effectively done in a straight-leg, flat-out position with your insteps hooked under the hiking strap and your thighs as far out on the rail as possible. Your body should be nearly horizontal over the water, and you should just be able to see your toes. Those who are in better condition will, of course, be able to hold this position longer.

On long courses, maintaining a straight-leg, flat-out position for entire weather legs can only be done by the most dedicated, well-conditioned Laser sailors. Most other sailors end up staying straight-legged, but with a more upright upper-body position. You should be able to hold the straight-leg, flat-out position for up to 10 minutes at a time. If that sounds like a short period of time, try it sometime. The best way to improve your endurance is to sail a lot and do plenty of leg exercises, sit-ups, and running.

It is just as important to be in good shape for reaching and running legs. If you are racing in light air, you will often need to assume awkward positions and will quickly realize that gains can be made by holding perfectly still. The better shape you are in, the easier it is to maintain such positions. In heavy air, you will find yourself constantly balancing the boat—trimming, steering, and keeping it flat. Flexibility and stamina are important for the dynamic moves required for good offwind sailing.

Naturally, you must have a set program to get yourself in top condition. Continuous practice in medium and heavy air will strengthen the ankle, shin, thigh, and stomach muscles, which are so important for long stints of hiking. This will also toughen hands and strengthen arm muscles for the constant sail adjustments required both on and off the wind, and will condition the body in general for the exhausting effort often required in tough, five-race weekend series.

If the weather and circumstances are not conducive to continuous practice, a physical conditioning program of off-the-water exercise must be developed and followed on a regular basis. The plan should be specifically designed to strengthen arm, thigh, and stomach muscles, toughen hands, and improve cardiovascular condition. Calisthenics, weight lifting, and the use of a hiking bench will improve muscle strength and tone. Running or skipping rope will improve cardiovascular fitness and endurance.

A hiking bench can easily be built, and is an excellent piece of equipment for conditioning if

Shaping up on the hiking bench: this exercise strengthens leg, abdomen, and arm muscles by hiking out—just as one would on the Laser—while pulling on the double simulated mainsheet.

you cannot sail all of the time because of climate or work or school responsibilities. The bench shown here actually simulates hiking in a Laser. The seat is the same width as the deck and the adjustable hiking strap is the same general height as the one in the Laser cockpit. A hiking bench like the one shown can be made in several hours at minimal expense. Vigorous pumping on the simulated mainsheet should be more than enough to raise a few blisters.

As part of a training program, start working on the bench at least two weeks before a regatta. Exercise about a half-hour a day, every other day. Hike as long and hard as you can, and pump the sheet 10 or 12 times with each hand. Rest days will give your hands a chance to toughen up, and your leg and stomach muscles time to rebuild.

It is quite possible to be out of breath and nearly exhausted at the end of a long reach or run in heavy air and rough seas in the Laser. Then cardiovascular conditioning, such as running or skipping rope, will give you the stamina to stay with it.

The more you race, the more you will discover that the leaders are always hiking harder and longer than the followers. You, too, will find that in competition, harder work will earn you more success.

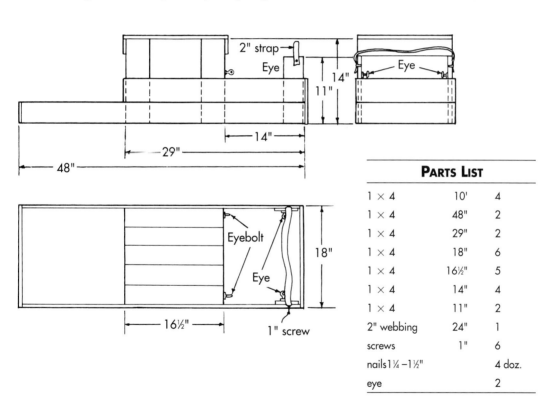

PARTS LIST		
1 × 4	10'	4
1 × 4	48"	2
1 × 4	29"	2
1 × 4	18"	6
1 × 4	16½"	5
1 × 4	14"	4
1 × 4	11"	2
2" webbing	24"	1
screws	1"	6
nails 1¼ –1½"		4 doz.
eye		2

EIGHT

Maintenance

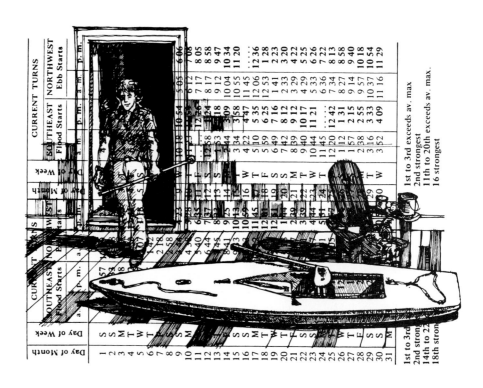

There are a number of stories about sailors who have picked up borrowed Lasers on the spur of the moment, most of the boats sadly lacking for care, and have gone on to win major championships. Carl Buchan raised eyebrows when he pulled a University of Washington club Laser off the rack and, in the next few days, went on to win a U.S. National Championship. A more extreme case occurred at a small regatta in New England where a sailor won in a Laser that had been stored under a pine tree for the past month. The bottom was splotched with clumps of sticky pine pitch.

Such incidents are the exception to the rule. Most Laser sailors, whether top-flight racers or simply proud owners, spend at least some time maintaining their boats. Keeping the hull clean or touching up accidental scratches and nicks may be all that will be required. The effort not only prolongs a Laser's life, but helps ensure good resale value.

Cleaning, Wet Sanding, and Polishing

Most foreign substances that tend to gather on the hull and deck come from trailering or cartopping the boat without a cover, or sailing in dirty and/or salt water. To clean the hull use a mild, nonabrasive detergent with a sponge or soft-bristle brush. For stubborn stains or particles, such as tar, use xylol or acetone. Don't allow acetone to remain on the hull for more than 30 seconds, as it can damage the fiberglass. After using the xylol or acetone, wash the area thoroughly with detergent.

The mast step should be kept especially clean. Any grit, sand, or salt left there will eventually be ground into the fiberglass walls of the step, impeding mast rotation and eventually causing leaks. Rinsing the boat while on its side will keep it clean. However, if the mast step hasn't been cleaned in some time, and the walls are looking black from the aluminum spar, scrub it out with a toilet bowl brush and some mild detergent, rinse well, and the step should look practically new. Application of Teflon mast antiwear strips can be helpful here also.

Those who race give their hulls an occasional light sanding with wet sandpaper, generally 400-, 600-, or 1000- grade. This cleans the hull and eliminates the "orange peel" surface often found on new boats. Some believe this produces a faster surface, although it does dull the gelcoat finish. If you do wet sand, be sure to back up the sandpaper with a sanding block to provide a more even surface than the unevenness of your hand. Don't overdo the sanding, especially in the mast step area; it is possible to sand through the gelcoat. If a dark-colored tinge appears in the area you are sanding, you are wearing through the gelcoat.

Like any fiberglass boat, Laser hulls will inevitably lose some of their original luster and shine if left exposed to the sun's ultraviolet rays for prolonged periods of time. To revitalize the hull cosmetically, polish it with a fine-grade polishing compound and follow that with a coat of wax. This will also make future cleaning easier.

However, if you race the boat, it is best not to use anything on the hull that has wax in it. As nice as it looks, a waxed hull has been found to be slower than an unwaxed one. Water will adhere to the microscopic roughness of a boat bottom, forming a thin layer that slides easily through adjacent water layers. A smoothly waxed hull, by contrast, repels water, creates bubbles, and causes turbulence. A polishing compound will bring back most of the luster. Be sure to check the contents, however, as some compounds contain wax while others do not. A good, new product is McLube, a dry lubricant that can be sprayed on the hull. Beware: this makes the hull so slippery that it can slide off the trailer!

Hull Repairs

The most important aspect of Laser hull maintenance is to make sure your boat remains watertight. Any water that gets into the hull and is left there tends to work its way into the foam core that reinforces the deck and the fiberglass, often adding considerable weight. Lasers that have not been kept dry, particularly older ones, have been known to weigh as much as 15 pounds more than dry hulls. That may not seem like much, but consider that it only takes two people to carry a 125- to 130-pound Laser around a parking lot; add 15 pounds to that, and it suddenly becomes necessary to have 3 people. More important, that excess weight seriously affects performance. Heavier boats react more sluggishly to helm movements and sail adjustments, are far less responsive to hiking and other crew movements, and are slower to plane and surf.

To ensure a dry hull, remove the transom drain plug after each sail and lift the bow at least waist-high to drain any water inside the boat. In extreme sailing conditions, it is not unusual to take on a cupful or so of water. But if there is much more than that, or you're taking on water after sailing in milder conditions, the leak(s) should be found and stopped.

Most hull leaks are small and almost impossible to see unless you know exactly where to look. To find them, cover any suspect area with a solution of soapy water. Common problem areas include where the deck and hull molds are glued together (not only around the rails, but also inside the centerboard trunk), mast step, cockpit bailer hole, around fittings, and, if you have them, inspection ports.

Once a suspect area has been covered with soapy solution, cover the air hole underneath the forward end of the hiking strap with tape. Air pressure introduced into the hull through the transom drain hole will cause bubbles to form where there are leaks. Air pressure can be created by blowing into the drain hole. A more efficient method, however, is to use a hair dryer or a vacuum cleaner, reversed, with the hose held several inches away from the hole. Don't put the hose right up to the hole, for you can possibly damage the hull by creating too much pressure. Once the leak is found, mark its location with a grease pencil, thoroughly dry the area, and seal with silicone sealant or epoxy. Remember to remove the tape over the air hole, as it is essential to stabilize the pressure within the hull.

If, after draining your hull of water and stopping the leak(s), the boat still seems considerably heavier than others (much over 130 pounds is considered heavy), it may be that water has been in the hull long enough to soak into the fiberglass and foam core. To dry it out, install a 6-inch, screw-on inspection port (bayonet ports are not only illegal, but tend to leak) in the middle of the stern deck and another a foot or so forward of the mast step. Now you have a path through which you can circulate warm, dry air in the hull to rapidly speed drying.

Once a circulation path is established, there are a number of methods to expedite drying. The simplest and most efficient way is to use a handheld hair dryer to create the necessary dry heat and a vacuum cleaner, reversed, to drive the heat through the boat. Be careful, for too hot a setting on the dryer may melt the fiberglass. Another method that works well, especially on your return from a sail on a hot summer day, is to car-top the boat and leave the inspection ports open, circulating air through the hull as you drive. A small "intake air scoop" attached to the bow inspection port will force even more air through the hull. The heat coming off the asphalt and car hood will get your boat bone-dry by the time you reach home.

Older Lasers that leak tend to be heavier than new boats that leak, often because older boats, built before 1974 or 1975, are equipped with foam flotation. This flotation consists of large Styrofoam blocks, one in the stern and several ahead of the cockpit, wrapped in plastic bags to ensure watertightness. However, after six or seven years, the bags begin to chafe on the insides of the hull. The Styrofoam is then exposed to moisture and will absorb it immediately. If, after installing inspection ports, you discover holes in the plastic bags, remove each bag and dry the blocks of Styrofoam. Then, put a new plastic bag around each block. You should be set for a few more years.

However, if the blocks are damp beyond salvaging, replace them with flexible, air-filled polyethylene containers, which can be carried inside the hull. This type of container is used in Lasers built since the mid-1970s. Available through your local Laser dealer, four 2½-gallon containers are carried in the stern and three 5-gallon ones ahead of the cockpit. The biggest installation problem is getting the old Styrofoam out through the inspection ports, generally accomplished by some patient chipping away at the Styrofoam with a knife or screwdriver. Once the air-filled containers are installed, you will have lightweight, reliable, nonabsorbent flotation.

Scratches

No matter how much care you give your Laser, the gelcoat will eventually get scratched. Cosmetic scratches, those almost indiscernible to the touch, can be eliminated by lightly sanding the area with wet sandpaper backed by a sanding block to ensure even sanding. Use 400-grade wet sandpaper, or even a finer grade. If a dark-colored tinge begins to appear, stop sanding; the tinge means you are wearing through the gelcoat and getting too close to the fiberglass beneath. After wet sanding, buff the area with a fine-grade polishing compound.

Deeper scratches and gouges can be easily felt and often go most of or all the way through the gelcoat, revealing the brownish-colored fiber-

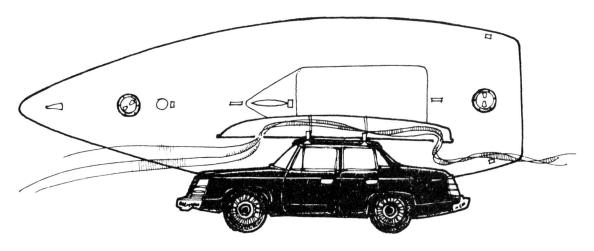

Inspection ports mounted bow and stern permit access to the hull's interior. They also permit the Laser to be dried out thoroughly. With ports unscrewed and the boat atop a car, a drying breeze is created.

glass beneath. For these you will first have to fill the damaged area with new gelcoat. Start by removing any loose particles of gelcoat with a knife or chisel and slightly bevel the undamaged gelcoat around it down toward the scratch or gouge. Then rough up the area, including a 1-inch surrounding area, with 60- to 80-grade dry sandpaper. The bevel and the rough surface will provide a more positive bond between the hull and the new gelcoat. Next, clean the section, preferably with acetone.

Now thoroughly mix the gelcoat for several minutes in a paper cup. Eventually a chemical reaction will begin producing enough heat to melt plastic or Styrofoam cups and make coffee cans difficult to hold. The warmer the ambient temperature, the faster the chemical reaction will occur. Allow the gelcoat to remain in its container for four or five minutes—just long enough to get the reaction going. Once it has started, evenly coat the damaged area with gelcoat, using a coffee stirrer or wood spatula. Add a little more gelcoat than you think necessary, for it shrinks slightly as it hardens. Gelcoat will not completely harden in the presence of air, so lay a strip of transparent tape over it. This also holds the patch in place. Once hardened, remove the tape, scrape off any excess gelcoat, sand and polish the scratch, and your repair should be almost invisible.

One section of the hull that is particularly susceptible to nicks and gouges is the gunwale. Such damage can be repaired in the same manner as damage to other parts of the hull, but the secret to creating a cosmetically acceptable gunwale patch is determined by how the gelcoat layer is taped. Attach the tape below the patch first, then fold it up over the area being repaired. The new patch will take on a shape virtually identical to the rest of the gunwale.

Punctures and Cracks

Although many people prefer to leave patching punctures and cracks to professionals, with a little care and planning repairs can be done in a home workshop. The main problem with repairing a punctured or cracked hull is the lack of access from inside. With a certain amount of dexterity, repairs can be done through a six-inch inspection port, assuming there is one close to the damaged area, or you can install one nearby.

To repair a puncture, first chip away any loose pieces of fiberglass and bevel and rough the edges of the good gelcoat around the area as you would for a scratch or gouge. Then, sand the area with 60- or 80-grade dry sandpaper and clean it with acetone. Next, cut out two pieces of 1-ounce fiberglass mat just large enough to cover the area of the puncture plus a 1-inch surrounding area.

If you can reach the hole through an inspection port, paint on polyester resin around the hole on the inside of the hull with a natural bristle brush. (Nylon bristles will melt from the heat caused by the resin's chemical reaction.) Then, thoroughly saturate one piece of the mat with resin and lay it in place inside over the hole, smoothing out any wrinkles or bubbles with the brush. Once the mat hardens, add another saturated piece from the outside of the hull. When this hardens, coat the patch with gelcoat and finish as you would a large scratch or gouge.

Patching a puncture without access to the inside of the hull is a little more complicated, but still possible (see illustration next page). Follow the same trimming, beveling, and cleaning methods outlined above. Using a small paint brush, reach through the puncture and coat the inside of the hull around the hole with resin. Use mat approximately 1 inch larger than the hole and cut a piece of cardboard slightly larger than the mat. Then saturate the mat and lay it on the cardboard. Thread three or four pieces of thin string, several feet long, through the cardboard and the mat, placing them as far apart as the hole will allow. Knot the string on the side of the cardboard opposite the side the mat is on. Tension on the strings will be used to hold the patch up against the inside of the hull. While the patch is still wet, fold the cardboard and mat together enough to slide them through and pull on the strings, drawing the patch up against the inside

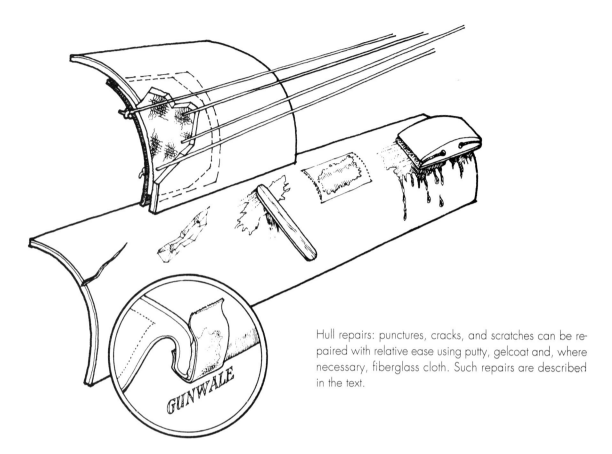

Hull repairs: punctures, cracks, and scratches can be repaired with relative ease using putty, gelcoat and, where necessary, fiberglass cloth. Such repairs are described in the text.

of the hull. Tie the strings to a nearby wall or other substantial object until the patch hardens. Then, cut the strings and patch the outside of the hull, as described above.

If you prefer not to leave the cardboard in the hull, it can be coated with mold-release or lined with wax paper before laying the mat on it. Attach an additional long string, this time only to the cardboard, and run it through the hole and to the nearest inspection port. Install the patch. Once the patch has hardened and you've cut the strings, pull the retrieval line separating the cardboard from the patch and draw the cardboard out of the hull.

Large hull cracks, usually created by a hard collision with a dock or another boat, are repaired much like punctures if there is an inspection port nearby. If there is no port handy, and the crack is

several inches long, cut the crack out; this will actually create a hole where there was once only a crack. Then, patch the hole using the cardboard backup method. If the crack is not that substantial, you can often get away with laying a piece of mat over the crack from the outside of the hull. When hardened, fair it in. Be careful not to sand the entire patch off, especially in the area of the crack itself. Afterward, coat the repair with a polyurethane-based paint.

If you discover a crack in your mast step, you can buy a repair kit from your Laser dealer containing a prefabricated mast step that you install after cutting out the existing one; you can also attempt to mend the present step. The former method, complete with instructions, does a fine job, and you will end up with a neat new mast step. The latter method requires a little improvisation, almost always works well, and is a good option for those without the heart for mast step surgery.

First, pinpoint the problem. If you suspect a leak, use the soapsuds and vacuum cleaner method described in the section on locating leaks. You will need access to that area from inside the hull, so install a 6-inch screw-in inspection port adjacent to the fault, a foot or so ahead of the mast step. Sand the entire mast step from inside the hull with 60- or 80-grade dry sandpaper, paying particular attention to the damaged section. Clean the step with acetone, then paint with epoxy. Tightly wrap the step with 1- to 3-inch-wide fiberglass mat in overlapping spirals from one end of the step to the other. Make sure the damaged area is especially well covered. If you have accurately located the leak and wrapped the step well, your mast step should be leak-proof and as strong as ever.

Spars

Spars are generally maintenance-free, but there are a few things you can do to keep them looking "like new." First, keep them as clean as possible. Saltwater sailors should be certain to rinse their spars with fresh water after every sail. For a more thorough cleaning, use a rubbing or polishing compound followed by a coat of wax. This helps prevent the spars from leaving a charcoal-colored discoloration on the sail sleeve and around the sail clew. It also permits the sail to slide on and off the spar much more easily and, when sailing, allows a more even and accurate cunningham adjustment along the sail luff. Racers often spray their cleaned spars with a silicone-based spray for the same reason.

It is especially important to keep the butt of the mast clean. This will allow the mast to rotate smoothly. Before you step the spar, run your hand over the bottom of it and make sure there is no dirt or grit there.

Occasionally check to make sure all mast and boom fittings are on securely. On the mast, check the gooseneck; the bolt that goes through the gooseneck pin may need tightening once in a while. It should be tight enough to prevent the pin from moving sideways, but not so tight as to prevent it from pivoting up and down. All rivets holding fittings on the mast or boom should be tight. If not, drill them out and replace them with equivalent-sized stainless steel rivets. It is best not to use aluminum rivets because, under stress, stainless steel fittings can shear them.

If your top and bottom spar sections fit together snugly, as they should, you might run into difficulties separating them when it comes time to take the boat apart. Former Laser class president Jack Couch often relishes watching three or four Laser sailors playing tug of war with a top and bottom section that appear to be stuck together permanently. He then bets them that his wife, Kiki, can separate the two sections all by herself. In just a few seconds longer than it takes them to put the spar down and her to pick it up, she has them apart! All she does is find a good solid edge, such as a concrete curb or a strong fence. Holding the top section, just down a bit from the end, she lays the bottom section over the edge so that the gooseneck fitting is pointing down and is located several feet beyond the far side of the edge. Then, in one fast tug, she pulls the entire mast toward her. In so doing, the gooseneck fitting snags on the edge, and the two stubborn sections pop apart.

To separate stuck mast sections, place mast so that gooseneck will catch on obstacle, and pull sharply.

Centerboards and Rudders

Boards and rudders are constructed of poly-urethane, self-skimming foam reinforced with high-tensile steel rods. Polyurethane boards are uniform in strength and surface, and they will not absorb water if cracked, chipped, or broken. However, they are sensitive to extreme temper-atures. If left in a car trunk or under a back seat window on a hot sunny day, the polyurethane may warp, especially if the temperature ap-proaches 175°F (80°C). They can also become brittle if the temperature drops down to −40°F (−40°C). Once warped, it is difficult but not im-possible to make them true again. They must be supported, placed in the reverse direction, and uniformly reheated to the point where they are once again straight. Remove the blade from the heat source and it should retain its shape. The sun is an excellent heat source. The process can be speeded up by placing a black trash bag over the blade. Observe the reaction carefully so as to not overdo the procedure.

One nice feature of the polyurethane boards is that they can be worked on with standard woodworking tools, including sandpaper and steel wool. Before starting, remember the loca-tion of the metal reinforcing rods. They lie only $\frac{1}{32}$ of an inch below the surface. Should one become exposed, coat it with epoxy before sailing. If one

of them has rusted, wire-brush all the rust off be-fore continuing with repairs.

Dents and scratches in the centerboard or rudder should be cleaned out and sanded with a 60- or 80-grade dry sandpaper, providing a rough surface for better adhesion. Clean the area with acetone, then fill with a polyester filler, which is available at auto body shops. Once hardened, sand the area smooth with increasingly fine wet sandpaper, starting with grade 320 and building to 400, then 600. Repaint the section with a polyurethane-based paint, and use at least one coat of primer and one of gloss. Finish by rubbing with auto body cutting paste. Treat any blisters in the outside skin the same way.

Almost all centerboard and rudder breakage is confined to the trailing edge. If the section is just cracked, fill with epoxy and clamp it in its normal position. Once the epoxy hardens, finish as you would for dents and scratches.

If a piece is entirely broken off and missing, as might happen to the lower front corner of the leading edge if you hit a rock at high speed, re-place the missing section with a piece of spruce or mahogany and epoxy glue. Make as accurate a fit as possible, which usually means squaring off the broken area of the board. Once fitted, finish as detailed above. Don't try to repair such sections with layers of body filler—it's good for about $\frac{1}{32}$ of an inch, but then becomes prone to cracking.

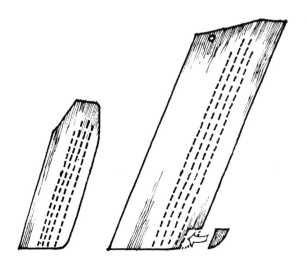

The Laser's centerboard and rudder are made of high-density polyurethane foam reinforced with high-tensile steel wires. Both board and rudder are subject to scratches and cracks, particularly at the edges. Broken pieces can be reattached with epoxy. Dents or cracks can be repaired with polyester filler. Should repairs re-quire the use of tools, be careful not to run into the rein-forcing wires. Their location is shown in the drawings.

Sails

The Laser sail is made of relatively lightweight material, which dictates careful handling. Most Laser sail care revolves more around what you do to the sail when you are not using it, rather than what you do with it when sailing. First, always

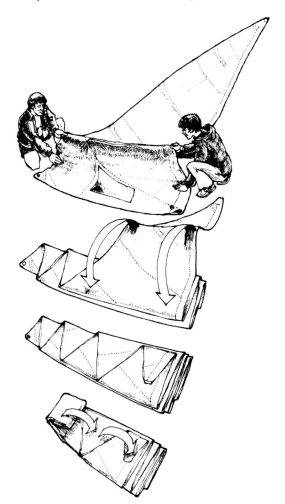

Care and feeding of the sail: the Laser's sail is made of high-quality Dacron and will last for years if given the proper care. The sail should be folded neatly after use, not just stuffed into the sail bag. Vary slightly the points at which you fold the sail to avoid permanent creases and do not crease the Mylar window. Sails can be washed in *cold* water with sail soap or mild detergent.

store the sail dry. Storing it wet can soften up the resin in the sail, allowing it to stretch more. If you've been sailing in salt water, make sure all of the salt is washed out when you're done sailing, as salt retains moisture. If the sail is soiled, wash with cold water and sail soap, or a mild detergent, and scrub with a soft-bristle brush. If really dirty, soak in a tub of soapy water for several hours to loosen the dirt. Never wash a sail in hot water or a washing machine, as that breaks down the sail's fibers. To clean the Mylar window, wipe with a soft, dry cloth and Plexiglas cleaner.

Some common sail stains that may be encountered are blood, mildew, and oil or tar. Bloodstains can be removed by mixing up a thick paste of dry detergent and water, and applying it to the area; it should be allowed to stand for about a half-hour. Then, rinse with warm water. If the stain persists, the only option left is to carefully bleach it out, being sure to completely rinse out the bleach afterward. For mildew, moisten the stain with warm, sudsy water with just a little bleach added. Then rinse and dry the area. Next moisten the stain again, this time with salt and lemon juice. Let it dry in the sun, and then rinse again with warm water.

Oil and tar present a more complicated problem. First gently scrape off any excess oil or tar with a spatula, being extremely careful not to cut the sail. Then, moisten a soft, absorbent cloth with dry-cleaning fluid. This will soak through the sail and carry the stain over onto the cloth. After you've eliminated as much of the stain as possible, clean the sail with mild detergent and rinse thoroughly.

Once the sail is clean, dry, and ready to put away, always fold it. The best method is "accordion" style, with each fold parallel to the foot. Prevent permanent creases by varying your folds from time to time and avoid folding across the window. Once folded into a long rectangle, fold the sail into a small square. Another method of sail storage is to roll it around the spar. This is fine as long as it is done loosely and the spar is clean and dry. The sail can also be loosely rolled, top to bottom, placed in a tube bag, and laid on a flat area for storage. Never store your sail by stuffing it, spinnaker-style, into its bag.

When the sail is up on the boat, there are mainly two things to avoid—unnecessary exposure to the sun's ultraviolet light and excessive flogging. Granted, both are integral parts of sailing, but try to minimize that kind of wear and tear on the sail. Allowing the sail to flap in the wind and sun for afternoons at a time breaks down the resin coating and stitching much more quickly than normal sailing use.

To participate in Laser regattas, you need numbers on the sail. The sail number should correspond to the number found on the hull. The examples and diagrams shown below indicate how the sail number system works. The numbers must be 12 inches high, 8 inches wide, and 1¾ inches thick. They must be positioned with 2⅜ inches between adjacent numbers, with the numbers on the starboard side placed above those on the port side. The first two numbers must be red. The last four numbers must be black.

These hints about Laser maintenance and repair are time-tested. Taking care of their boats is something most sailors seem to enjoy. Certainly, the more familiar you are with maintaining the Laser, the better you'll understand the boat as a whole. You'll probably even become a better sailor for the shoreside time spent in keeping your boat's hull, spars, and sail in top shape.

Serial number SLI C3456, Sail number 123456
The "C" preceding the four-digit number on the hull indicates that the boat is in the 120,000 to 120,999 range of serial numbers. A=10 B=11 C=12 D=13 E=14 F=15 etc . . .

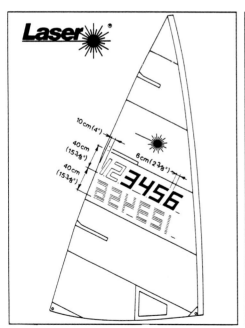
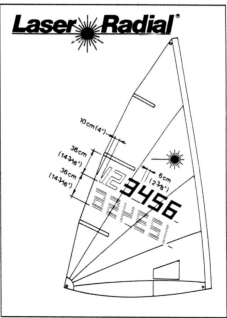

Applying sail numbers: to participate in Laser regattas, you need numbers on the sail. The sail number should correspond to the number found on the hull. The numbers must be 12 inches high, 8 inches wide, and 1¾ inches thick. They must be positioned exactly as shown with 2⅜ inches between adjoining numbers, with the number on the starboard side placed above that on the port side.

NINE

Trailering, Cartopping, and Storage

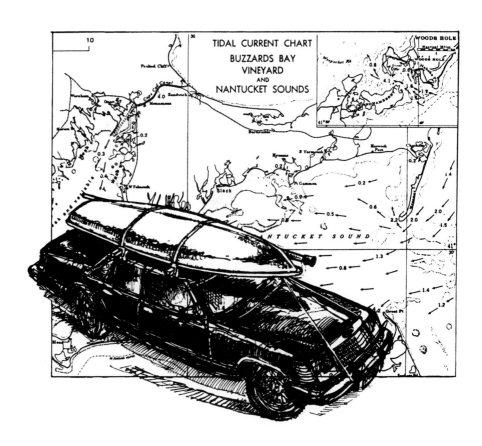

There's a Warren Miller movie that begins with a shot of a yellow Laser atop a fast-moving station wagon on a winding mountain road. All of a sudden, the bow begins to lift, and the boat flies back on its transom and goes spinning off the car. Miller's omnipresent camera follows the boat closely as it crashes, stern first, onto the edge of the road, then goes careening end over end down a brushy embankment where it eventually comes to rest in a cloud of dust after traveling down almost 350 feet of vertical drop. "The only damage done to the boat," said Miller, "was that when it hit the pavement, it landed on the starboard quarter. That left a ding in it about as big as your thumb, and that was it. With a little gelcoat and filler, it was fixed in about an hour."

Although that incident indicates the Laser's strength, the damage could certainly have been worse had it landed somewhere besides a stern quarter. And, as Miller pointed out, had it been an unstaged situation with oncoming traffic, the yellow Laser could have easily become a lethal weapon. Transporting the Laser, as simple as it may seem, is something to be carefully thought out, not only for your convenience and the protection of the boat, but also for the safety of other drivers.

Trailering

Since the Laser is relatively light, at about 130 pounds, few sailors actually launch their boats from the trailer, as do owners of larger boats. In-stead, they lift them off the trailers and carry them down to the water, or use small, commercially made dollies. Peter Seidenberg's Seitech Dolly is by far the most popular. Many regatta sailors strap a Seitech Dolly upside down on the bottom of their boat, which in turn is either strapped on a trailer, or on Thule or Yakima car-top racks. Use of these dollies avoids marring the hull's finish by sliding it over trailer rollers or bunkers, plus it saves wear and tear on the trailer wheels and bearings, particularly around salt water.

Since most Laser trailers never get wet, they can be used for more than simply transporting the hull. Some sailors have designed trailers that not only have room for the hull and spars, but also feature boxes to store all the other equipment needed for sailing—everything from rudders, centerboards and sails to life jackets, wet suits and cleaning supplies. This not only leaves more room in the car, but also makes packing for a regatta or a simple afternoon sail much easier—all you have to do is hook the trailer to the car and go!

When setting up a trailer, keep in mind two major functions: first, protection of the boat from road dirt, tar and stones; second, proper hull support to effectively hold the boat on the trailer and prevent undue stress on the hull when traveling on rough roads.

If the trailer is to carry the boat right side up, the best setup is to build a form-fitting, padded bunker for the aft end and a thick pad for the bow

Laser trailers: the double-decker trailer **(1)** features separate cradles for each hull (carried upside down) along with plastic drainage tubing for the spar sections. Centerboards, rudders, tillers, sails, and even sailing clothing is all stored in the rectangular boxes, which also serve to protect the hulls from stones and dust kicked up by passing cars. On the single-Laser trailer **(2)**, the hull is carried upside down, well away from the road surface. Spars fit neatly in the hull bunker cutouts and all other equipment can easily fit into the box. Note the air vent in the middle of the box's side to allow wet gear to dry.

to rest on. The two strongest sections of the boat are the areas just under the mast step and under the aft bulkhead of the cockpit right at the cockpit drain hole. Arrange the bunker and bow pads accordingly. If your trailer has pads running fore and aft and you don't wish to retrofit it to specifically fit your Laser, make sure the pads are located at the turn of the bilge, where the bottom curves into the topsides. Remember, any fiberglass hull left sitting on improperly designed or positioned supports can easily be deformed. So, check frequently to ensure that your boat is resting properly on its supports. To keep the hull dust-free and protect it from road tar, use a hull cover.

Once suitably supported, use two wide straps (at least 1 to 2 inches wide) to tie the boat down. Pass one over the mast step and the other over the aft cockpit bulkhead. Soft, large-diameter line can also be used. Cinch the lines tight by using truckers knots, placing a pad on the edges of the boat under the lines. Finally, secure the boat to prevent fore-and-aft movement.

Many Laser sailors prefer to carry their boats upside down on trailers, a method with several distinct advantages. Most important, it protects the bottom of the hull from anything thrown up by the tires, such as stones, dirt or tar. Granted, the deck and inside of the cockpit will receive the brunt of this damage, but for many that is far preferable to exposing the bottom. Another advantage is that this arrangement does not require any special bunkers, for the boat will be resting on its relatively flat deck. There is some curvature to the deck, however, so it is best to add a little extra padding along the area where the outer edge of the deck sits. Run wide straps across the mast step and cockpit drain hole areas, and tie the bow down to the trailer.

Spars can be lashed onto the trailer alongside the boat. Be careful to position them, however, so they don't rub against the boat. If trailering your Laser right side up, the spars can also be lashed together and then tied onto the deck, provided there is padding between spars and deck. Spar Partners (foam blocks), made by Ken Hopkins of Nautical America, are designed for this purpose.

It is also possible to trailer two or three Lasers together. There are a number of methods for doing this. All are satisfactory as long as each boat is properly supported and the trailer is not overloaded. For temporary two-boat trailers, the simplest method is to put the bottom boat on right side up with some padding on the tip of the mast step and aft of the cockpit bulkhead, and then place the second boat upside down on top of the first. Lash the two boats together, then lash the entire unit to the trailer. Keep in mind that when stacking boats on a trailer, the bottom boat will bear the weight of all others, so limit the stack to no more than three boats.

If you are traveling or sailing by yourself, it is possible to launch a Laser single-handedly with a Kitty Hawk or Trailex trailer. These trailers are designed to both transport and launch Lasers. They are light enough so that they can be removed from the towing vehicle and hand-pushed into water deep enough to float the Laser off. The boat can be recovered in the same manner. Using Bearing Buddies on the wheels will facilitate regreasing the wheel bearings. If you are launching in salt water or prefer not to immerse the trailer in the water, then the use of a Seitech Dolly is an excellent alternative. This dolly can be easily carried upside down on top of the Laser while traveling and facilitates the launching and recovering manuevers. Place your Seitech Dolly 60–90 degrees from the boat and trailer with the bow ends nearly touching each other. Lift the Laser off the trailer by the transom, pivot it and place it over the Seitech Dolly. Set the stern down on the dolly. Then walk up to the bow and lift it off the pivot and onto the dolly. Roll the dolly and boat to the launching area. Reload in reverse manner. If you are using a conventional or standard trailer, and have no one to assist you, you can perform the same procedure by placing the Seitech Dolly directly behind the trailer. Slide the Laser aft onto the dolly and launch.

Spiling means transferring a curved shape, such as a hull section, onto a template that can then be used for cutting out the shape. Using the spiling method shown here, one can duplicate the shape of a Laser's bottom and make a cradle for storage or transport. An alternative way to create a cradle that will match the hull's shape is to use the offsets shown here, drawing vertical lines at the specified intervals to specified heights. The lines are then joined, using a long flexible batten to help make a fair curve.

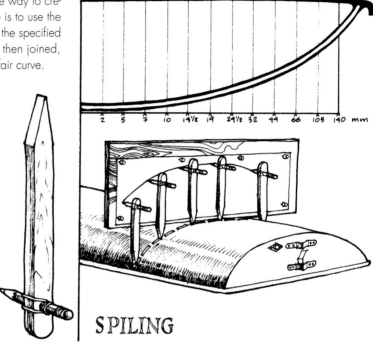

OFFSETS

SPILING

Cartopping

The most popular method by far of transporting Lasers is on top of a car. Roof racks are less expensive than trailers, support the boat just as well, and do not subject the boat to nearly as much road damage.

When selecting a rooftop rack, it is most important to check a manufacturer's specifications to ensure the rack will support the weight of the boat and spars. The most commonly used racks are Thule and Yakima.

Unless you have a large vehicle, you will be unable to put the roof racks directly under both the mast step and aft cockpit bulkhead. As a compromise, center the boat as best you can over the car, making sure it hangs out over both ends

equally. Then add padding to the racks so the boat's weight is spread over as large an area as possible. This usually means adding a little extra padding at the front and back ends of the racks. As in trailering, lash the boat down with several wide straps. To prevent fore-and-aft movement, tie the bow eye to the front of the car and tie the back of the boat to the rear.

If you are by yourself and need to load and unload your Laser from the top of the vehicle, a Seitech Dolly can be used here too. Place the dolly behind your vehicle, bow pointing to the rear. Slide the Laser off the back of the vehicle (use a well-cushioned rear support), stand it on its transom (use a soft pad on the ground) in a straight-up position. Quickly move around the boat and carefully lower it onto the dolly. This

Kitty Hawk (shown above) and Trailex trailers are lightweight, around 100 pounds, have submersible lights and three-point gunwale supports which prevent hull deformation. They can be used as dollies for launching and towed at highway speeds. They have pivoting bow supports for easy single-handed offloading and loading or for transferring to a Seitech Dolly for launching and recovery.

can be precarious, especially in a strong wind, and should be considered as a last-resort procedure.

It is possible to stack several Lasers on top of a car, but this is generally a rather precarious situation: it is difficult to support the hulls properly and can be quite a lift to get the top boat up in position. A more common traveling method for two Lasers is to put one on top of the car and the second on a trailer that has a storage box. That way, all of the gear can go in the box, saving room in the car. In addition, if only one boat is needed, either can be selected without having to move both around.

Storage

The first rule of Laser storage, particularly in areas where the temperature drops below freezing, is to make sure there is no water in the hull. Over a prolonged period of time, water can be absorbed into the hull. During freezing winter temperatures, that water can freeze and expand, causing definite damage. Once any water is drained,

Left: Seitech Dolly facilitates launching and recovery. **Below:** For single-handed launching and retrieving, the Laser and its dolly can be carried together on a conventional trailer.

leave the transom plug out and any inspection ports open, allowing the hull to dry out during storage.

If you are dry-sailing at a boat club or dinghy park, be sure your Laser is properly stored between sails. Never leave it on anything that will hold moisture up against the hull, such as wet sand or carpet. Moisture held against the hull for prolonged periods will damage the finish.

Never store a Laser right side up on a flat rack or the lightly built hull will lose its shape. Make sure the rack is shaped to correctly support the hull under the mast step and the cockpit's aft bulkhead. The same holds true for hull cradles. And, unless stored in a sheltered location, pass one or two straps over the boat to make sure it isn't lifted off and damaged in a heavy wind.

If you're short on space, sit the hull up on its side against a wall, so it is resting on the gunwale. Put padding under the gunwale in several places to evenly spread the load and give the boat a little more stability. Also, pad between the boat and the wall. To store two or more Lasers in a confined area, stack them in a row, on their sides, with each boat resting on its gunwale and gently leaning up against the boat stacked just before it. Put padding between each Laser where one boat leans up against another.

A common storage method used when not at a boat club and space is limited, particularly in a garage, is to suspend the boat from the ceil-

Top: Lasers stored on transoms at the U.S. Naval Academy.
Bottom: Deck storage racks.

Lasers stored on gunwales in racks.

ing. This can be done right side up or upside down. In either case, use wide strapping to spread the load, and run it over the mast step and cockpit drain plug sections.

For spars, sail, centerboard, rudder, and loose gear, simply store indoors. If you sail in salt water, be sure to thoroughly rinse this equipment before storing for any length of time. It's a good feeling to know that the next time you're ready for a sail, your equipment will be in good condition and ready to go.

TEN

Sportsmanship

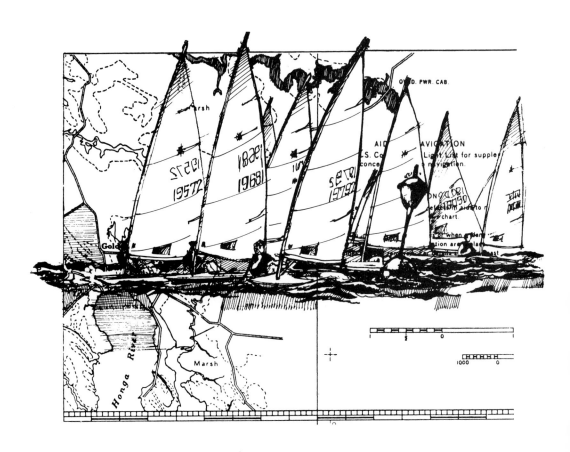

Fair and Friendly Competition

Since so much of this book has dealt with racing, it seems proper to include some comments about sportsmanship. In my opinion, racing small boats is the ultimate combination of mental and physical skills. Sailors seek an ever-increasing level of competition and derive tremendous satisfaction when they are able to beat those whom they consider better than themselves. The greatest satisfaction goes to those who win fair and square. It is much better to win by sailing faster than by altering the boat unfairly or by registering a questionable protest. Winning by using a standard boat with standard equipment is better than outspending and "out-gadgeting" the competition. With the Laser there is no choice. The few changes allowed by the rules are for making the boat more enjoyable or comfortable to sail and race.

Everyone enjoys friendly rather than cutthroat competition. The spirit of sportsmanship should always prevail. I remember vividly a few examples from way back which illustrate this spirit. In one race at the 1959 Snipe World Championship, we were caught on the starting line on port tack in light air, bobbing up and down with no steerage, when the gun fired. A competitor with good momentum was coming toward us on starboard tack. Rather than tag us out, he bore off slightly and purposefully avoided us, expecting nothing in return. The individual was Paul Elvström, who already at that time had won four Olympic Gold Medals.

Later, at the 1966 European Finn Championship, I loaned an extra stopwatch to a Russian competitor, Valentin Mankin. He more than repaid the favor two years later by loaning me his own mast when he observed that I had poor boat speed. His generosity and sportsmanlike attitude, crossing international and political boundaries, will always be remembered. He has won two Olympic Gold medals.

Another time, in a local Snipe regatta, we lost our whisker pole on a reach. We sailed the next run holding the jib out, and lost several places. With another race yet to go we were in poor spirits, until a competitor offered us his spare pole. I am sure that he got as much or more satisfaction in the giving as we did in the receiving.

These are only three acts of sportsmanship I have witnessed. Other sailors, I am sure, can recall as many or more. The satisfaction in racing comes from doing your best, improving with practice, and helping each other enjoy close racing by clean and fair sailing. Cut your competitors a little slack on the race course if necessary. A small duck when on starboard tack is not going to hurt anybody. A little extra room around the mark will be greatly appreciated. No doubt the concession will be returned more than once. Be sure to know and understand the International Racing rules. Laser sailors can be competitive without being confrontational and loud. Courtesy

101

on the course will go a long way toward promoting Laser class growth.

As far as Laser class rules are concerned, each Laser owner should know the rules, especially the object of the rules, which states, "The Laser is a strict one-design dinghy where the true test, when raced, is between helmspersons and not boats and equipment." The class rules cannot cover every possibility concerning material changes to a Laser. The intent, however, is clear, and the boat's one-design character will be protected at every level for the enjoyment of those who want a Laser for what it is.

Enjoy Yourself

I have been racing small sailboats and windsurfers for many years. During this time, I have never lost enthusiasm for competitive racing, and it is always fun to compete. Still, it is more fun to win, so I hope this book will help you sail Lasers faster and better, and through sportsmanship and fair sailing, enjoy the sport to the fullest. Reading and studying the following interviews of champion sailors will be of further benefit to the serious sailor. Good luck.

ELEVEN

Interviews

Since the Laser's creation, a number of sailors have become known for their expertise in the boat. Following are interviews with 12 well-known Laser sailors: Hans Fogh, Peter Commette, Danielle and John Myrdal, Ed Baird, Tom Lihan, Terry Neilson, John Bertrand, Lainie Pardey, Dave Olson, Ed Adams, and Luther Carpenter. Each shares his or her experience and ideas regarding a specific aspect of Laser sailing. Their thoughts will interest anyone wanting to better understand the boat or improve his or her performance on the race course.

The Story Behind the Laser Radial

HANS FOGH

Few sailors have a more enviable racing record than Hans Fogh, who has participated in six Olympics, sailing the Flying Dutchman and Soling. Hans won a Silver Medal in 1960 and a Bronze Medal in 1984, which is the longest span between two Olympic medals in any

sport. He has also won three world championships, one as a crew member uboard fellow Danish skipper Paul Elvström's Soling and two sailing his own Flying Dutchman. And he has logged a host of other major championships, ranging from European Championships and U.S. Nationals to Kiel Week and CORK. But, particularly in the Laser's early years, Fogh figured significantly in class growth, working with Bruce Kirby on the rig and sail plan and often finishing in the top 10 in major Laser events. In early 1982, he unveiled his own Laser Radial rig, a spar and sail combination for the Laser hull that he hoped would open the Laser class up to an even broader spectrum of sailors by catering to the class lightweights. The Laser story continues with Fogh's innovative design, which has proven most successful.

When did you first conceive the concept of a Laser Radial rig?

It took about two years; I believe I started working on it around 1979.

What prompted your interest in creating a new rig for the Laser?

I've always felt the Laser was a tremendous boat, but to compete at the top of the class, you've got to be 175 pounds or more and absolutely strong. A light person, or someone who cannot put a lot of time into training, really doesn't have much of a chance against such people. It also interested me because, at the time, I had two boys who had started out in Optimist dinghies and were ready to take the next step up. They were getting into Laser sailing, but at only 14 years old and being pretty light in weight, they just couldn't hold the boat down. And there really wasn't anything else but two-person boats. There's nothing wrong with that, but I felt maybe the Laser could suffice if the rig was redesigned. So I believed there was a real hole in the market for that size sailor. I figured that if I could come up with a rig that had the right bending characteristics, a 120- to 150-pound person could be comfortable sailing the boat, even in a 15- to 20-mph wind. I also knew that there were about 20,000 Optimist sailors in Europe just waiting for such a boat. It's there that the market is potentially the strongest. The European Optimist sailors just don't have anything to move up to other than the Laser, which is too much boat. They can go into the European Moth, which is a nice little boat, but it costs a lot more than the Laser. My idea was that the Laser has done everything possible, but there are a lot of secondhand boats out there that could be sailed. By adding a radial rig at the expense of just a few hundred dollars, they could borrow or buy one of those Lasers and end up with a very inexpensive new class.

But didn't the Laser M fit that need? It was within a couple of square feet of sail area as the Laser Radial.

The M had the same bottom section as the standard Laser, but a shorter top section. Therefore the rig was very stiff. At the same time, the M sail also had a very low aspect ratio. That means there was a lot of diagonal stretch in the sail. Also, the sail panels were quite big. So when the wind came up, all of that added up and the sail actually got baggier because you couldn't bend any of the fullness out with the mast, and the boat was tough to handle.

What did you do to create a spar with different bending characteristics?

The bottom section of the Radial is of a different design than either the standard Laser or the Laser M. A regular Laser section simply cut 2 feet shorter wouldn't work as well because its thick walls make it very stiff. I started by experimenting with a lot of different lengths. I tried a longer top section and a very short bottom section, and many other combinations, but was never happy with any of them. One day, I took the bottom section, cut 2 feet off it and took it into a hydraulic press. I flattened out the bottom section, between the gooseneck and the vang attachment, so that it was oval shaped—making it stiff sideways but with more fore-and-aft bend. It was only flattened about half the spar's thickness and over a distance of about a foot. I put it together with a top section and the boat just took off.

You mean the boat felt a lot better to sail than the M or any of your other spar experiments?

Yes. I had made the bottom section bend nicely. That gave the boat a good helm. If the mast had been left stiff fore and aft, there would have been no helm in the boat because the sail's center of effort would stay forward. But if the mast bends aft at the deck, as this one did, it creates enough helm to carry a smaller sail.

How did the rig respond in puffs?

When a puff came, the mast bent more and the sail leech opened up. I didn't need the weight to hold the boat flat, nor did I have to work as hard hiking to hold it down. I immediately called up Ian Bruce at Performance Sailcraft and said, "Look! Now it's working." And Ian said, "Okay, I'll find a bottom section that has the same bending characteristics as the section you pressed out." He came up with one that was very light, had thinner walls and bent very easily over the deck. In diameter, though, it is the same size as a standard bottom section so it fits the hull mast step.

With the thinner walls, did you anticipate any structural problems, particularly around the gooseneck area?

That was a concern. To be sure it wouldn't break there, Ian sleeved a piece of metal inside the spar to reinforce the area where the gooseneck goes on.

Why did you select a radial-cut sail?

Many years ago, I sailed with a radial-cut sail in the Flying Dutchman class, and we won an Olympic silver medal with it in 1960. At the time, I was working for Paul Elvström, and we used the radial cut because it stabilized the leech so that it never hooked—it was always open and straight. We were especially happy with it in heavy air. Since a lot of sailmaking goes in cycles—one idea or method falls by the wayside for a while but reappears a few years later—I've always kept the success of the radial cut in the back of my mind. Also, I considered the characteristics of the small-boat sailcloth being manufactured today. Most of the cloth is warp-oriented. In other words, it is strongest in the direction the panel is running rather than from the top of the panel to the bottom. That's largely an economic matter, because it costs much more to shoot in extra fill threads—those running from the top of the panel to the bottom. To get the most out of that type of cloth, you really need a radial cut, which aligns the warp with the leech rather than perpendicular to it.

Specifically, what type of cloth did you end up using for the Radial?

It was a 3.9-ounce Bainbridge cloth, which worked out very, very well. I thought that we would have to have an inexpensive cloth to keep the cost of the rig down, but I also wanted a cloth as high-quality as possible. With the right cut, it performed well. Plus, it allowed some re-

ally new and smart color combinations. But it wasn't just a fashion story; we looked at many aspects.

Did you have any other considerations when you were trying to tailor the Laser Radial to lightweight people?

In a breeze, one of the problems small people have always had is coming up with enough strength to raise the rig. So I put a halyard on the rig. There's a cup-shaped piece of cloth with a fairlead sewn on the end of it. The cup fits over the upper end of the top section, and the halyard goes through it. You then sleeve the sail on the spar, pushing it well down the mast, attach the halyard, and with the sail only part way up, the rig can be more easily raised. Once the mast is up, the sail can be hoisted and the halyard cleated off at the gooseneck area of the spar. I made sure to include enough space in the sail luff tube so the sail could be lowered easily and a long way down.

But now the Radial doesn't use a halyard.

Around the mid-nineties, it was decided to change the Radial halyard system back to the way the regular Laser did it. The reason was because of inconsistency in halyard tension and it made it simpler and easier to sail. They also changed from the color sail combination to plain white sails. The inconsistency in colored sailcloth forced the class to go to plain white cloth because of a more consistent spec. This has helped to equalize the sails.

How does the Laser Radial sail have to be trimmed compared to a Laser sail with a horizontal cut?

It doesn't really have to be trimmed that much differently because the shape of the sail is locked in. However, the most important adjustment, other than the mainsheet, is the outhaul. That's because all of the panels are joined to the clew. When you pull the clew aft with the outhaul, it's like a jib on a big boat—as you tighten it, the sail becomes flatter in the back and at the bottom. That's good for lightweight sailors because it makes a fairly dramatic change in the sail, and they can easily make that adjustment. So the outhaul is very critical.

Will the sail have to be vanged as hard as a standard Laser?

It's hard to say, but I think the short traveler on the boat affects the vanging process more than the sail cut does. When you don't have much traveler, as you ease the mainsheet, the boom goes up as well as out. The vang prevents it from going up.

In other words, vang sheeting?

That's right.

How about the cunningham? Is it anywhere as sensitive as the outhaul?

No. It is sensitive, but not nearly as much as the outhaul. It can be adjusted pretty much like the cunningham on the Laser.

What was the initial response to the Laser Radial?

In December 1982, I talked with a dealer in Miami, Florida, and he bought 20 sails. He sold 10 the first week and the next 10 shortly after that. My projection was that by 1991 there would be 50,000 Laser Radials. I think it appealed to even more people than the standard Laser. That's because it's easy to hike, and, like the original Laser, it's a lot of fun to sail. It's also an inexpensive way to get competitive. I really don't want to see anybody have to spend a lot of money to become a world-class sailor.

Hans, it is now nearly 10 years after your prediction of 50,000 Laser Radials by 1991. Rarely has there been an opportunity in sailing to tally up and reflect on a 10-year projection on something so innovative. How close did you come?

The reason I made that prediction was because I felt so enthusiastic about the boat—a little too enthusiastic as it turned out, but my feeling for the boat has not changed. The Europe Dinghy was chosen as the Olympic boat for women which affected the growth of the Laser Radial. How close I came in my prediction is difficult to say, but I know many thousands of people have enjoyed the Laser Radial. It has now been exactly 17 years since the Laser Radial came on the market; I know that it is still up-to-date with its mast and sail combination for the lightweight crew and also a great training boat for men and women before they step into the Laser.

A Look at the Laser Past

PETER COMMETTE

Unquestionably, one of Laser racing's greats is Peter Commette. Growing up in the Mantoloking (New Jersey) Yacht Club program racing M-Scows and later at Tufts University under the tutelage of sailing coach Joe Duplin, Commette scored a decisive win at the first Laser Worlds in 1974. He finished a close second at the third Laser Worlds in 1977 after taking a year off to train for the Kingston Olympics, where he represented the U.S. in the Finn class.

In the last twenty years, Commette has stopped racing Lasers seriously but has raced Snipes (North American Champion, 1992 and National Champion, 1996), and has updated his initial interview with his personal thoughts. Being part of the Laser scene from the onset allows him a unique perspective on the class history.

When did you first start sailing Lasers?

In the summer of 1971, just going into my senior year of college at Tufts. My family was in the market for a Sunfish or a similar boat. One day, a guy named Skip Moorehouse was demonstrating the Laser at our yacht club. It was in the size range we were interested in. My dad took one look at it, saw how well it sailed, and decided it was superior to anything else we'd seen. He bought it on the spot—boat number 246.

Did you immediately start racing the boat?

There wasn't much racing at that point. The Laser's first major event was the North Americans, sailed that October in Baltimore. That first summer we had the boat, I don't think I ever sailed upwind. I just reached back and forth in front of our house. Then I heard someone say they were going to start racing these things, so a friend of mine, Roy DeCamp, and I decided we had better see how they sailed upwind. We went for about 5 or 10 minutes upwind, stopped, and started reaching back and forth again, convinced that these boats would just never make it. They were simply too hard to sail upwind.

So how did you finally start racing?

I'd been racing most of my life in other boats, and since we had a Laser, and there were eventually other Lasers to race, I decided it was the natural thing to do. I'd also been racing an M-Scow, and still had that boat. I found it really wasn't too much of an ordeal to go to all of the regattas for each boat.

So was your first major event the North Americans that fall?

That's right.

What were your impressions of that event?

Dick Tillman won that championship, and of course, I was real impressed with him. He was a quiet guy who just hiked harder than everyone else. He also just seemed to be able to sail right through the fleet in every race.

As you got into racing Lasers back then, what

things were talked about as keys to making the boat perform well?

The biggest concern was staying upright when sailing offwind, particularly in heavy air. We used to say that, if you didn't tip over, you won the race. If you only tipped over once, you would probably be second. As far as adjustments go, one focus of a lot of attention was the traveler. Now of course, you must keep it tight most of the time. But then, people were coming from classes like the Snipe, and experimenting with all types of traveler tension. They were also setting the cunningham up with a 2:1 purchase, which today is hardly minimal for even recreational sailors. There was also a big question about whether or not to tie the clew down. We were doing all sorts of things that most Laser sailors take for granted today.

What kind of an effect did the change in sails from the Elvström to the computer-cut in 1974 have on the class?

For a while, people thought the newer sails were not quite as good as the Elvströms. What happened was the Elvströms got bigger and bigger over time. I'm not quite sure how that worked, but I understand it had to do with how they cut the patterns. So the newer sails tended to be a bit smaller. In addition, the Elvströms were made of different cloth than the new sails, and the Elvströms seemed to have an edge there. They set nicely on the spars. As a result, for a while, we all went around hoarding the old Elvströms.

After winning the first Worlds in Bermuda in 1974, you took a year off for the Olympics, missing the 1976 Worlds in Kiel, Germany, then returned for the 1977 Worlds in Brazil, where you finished a close second to John Bertrand. What differences did you see in the competition between the 1974 and 1977 Worlds?

Going into the 1977 Worlds, it had been about two years since I really sailed the Laser. Just before those Worlds, I went to the Nationals in Fort Lauderdale, which I won. Bertrand was second. What I noticed there was that everybody was good—really good. Even the kids were good. In Bermuda, it was fairly easy to work your way out of the middle of the fleet. In fact, in the last race, I was over early at the start and had to come back from last, which I did. But based on what I'd seen at the Nationals, I was pretty sure I wouldn't be able to do anything like that in Brazil. Sure enough, what I found in Brazil was that the guys at the top were sailing as well as usual, but in the middle, the boats were being sailed a whole lot better. And from just watching a number of Laser races lately, I think the caliber of racers has improved not only in the middle, but in the bottom of the fleet as well.

What kinds of changes have you noticed in the people who race Lasers?

In the old days, people could just hop into the class and end up near the top. You just can't do that anymore. You really have to know the boat to do well. Another change is the age of the people racing the Laser. The kids are a lot younger. But that's just as good, for it's benefited the class in many ways. I got into the Laser at age 17. Along with collegiate sailing, the Laser had helped turn me into a good sailor by the time I was 19. Many of these kids are starting in Lasers at 9 or 10. By the time they get a little seasoning in the class, and by the time they reach their late teens, they'll be really good sailors. I was down at the Coral Reef Sailing Club a while back, and there were some very good new Laser sailors there—Morgan Reeser, Tom Lihan, and a few others. They're talking about the same stuff I was talking about when I was 22 or 23, only they are talking about it at ages 17 and 18.

Looking back on all the Laser sailing you have done, does any one incident stand out?

The Laser's given me a lot of good memories, and it's difficult to pick out which is the best. But one of the most unusual situations happened to Ian Bruce and me at the Worlds in Brazil. The prevailing winds were out of the east, which created huge waves that would wash underneath you on starboard tack. On one leg, I found myself about 20 feet directly behind Ian. I've always looked up to Ian and enjoyed sailing against him, but never liked being behind him. So I was intent on catching him. All of a sudden, this huge wave came in and broke right on top of Ian's boat, grabbing it, and moving it about 50 feet to leeward. In an instant, I went from being 20 feet directly behind him to being the same distance behind him, but 50 feet further to windward. I'll never forget the look on his face. Once ashore, he wanted me to verify what had happened. Other than that, some of the best times I've had in a Laser were simply going out and practicing with a bunch of friends. We'd go out in real heavy air and just go back and forth all day, constantly sparring with each other.

Who would you regard as your toughest Laser competition over the years?

It's hard to say. The sailors whom I thought were the best I have sailed against are probably Carl Buchan and John Bertrand.

What distinguishes them from other excellent sailors in the class?

They never roll over and die. They always come at you, they can always recover when they are in the tank, and you really have to sail your best to beat them. There isn't a point of sail they can't do well on. And they both have a lot of savvy—they are always hustling, always pushing, always trying to get that extra inch around the race course. Those are the types of people that are tough to beat. When I sail against them, I often have the least success, but the most fun.

Your last major Laser regatta was the 1980 Midwinters. What happened there?

I lost to Ed Baird in the final leg of the last race in medium to light air. He hammered me. The wind was flukey with a lot of traffic around the leeward mark. I didn't cover early up the leg, and the rest is history. Ed won. I was second.

Why haven't you been active in the Laser in the last twenty years since the 1980 Midwinters?

Let me first say that I have an active *interest* in Lasers that will never die. Sailing Lasers was a special part of my life and the Laser is a special boat, maybe one of the purest extensions of the human body for sailing. I love the boat, and I loved the Laser experience. I just can't get back in it. I don't have the time or the body to do it

at the top anymore, and if I can't sail a Laser at the top, I just don't want to sail it.

Why not Laser Masters regattas?

I like sailing against the best. It's ten years since I became a Master. Back when I first became a Master, it made no sense. There just wasn't deep competition. Now that others have qualified for Masters competitions, I may do it.

Sailing and Training Together
DANIELLE MYRDAL AND JOHN MYRDAL

John Myrdal, 1998 U.S. Olympic Committee Sailing Athlete of the Year, three-time Collegiate Sailing All-American (1991–94), and ranked among the top three of the U.S. Sailing Team in Lasers, is training for the 2000 Olympics with his wife, Danielle. Danielle Brennan Myrdal, a four-time Women's All American Sailing Team member (1994–98), 1994 Rolex Yachts-woman of the Year, and runner-up in the 1994 ISAF World Single-Handed Women's Sailing Championship, is seeking an Olympic berth in the Europe Dinghy. Together, they are training in these two classes and share the latest thinking on training and sailing the Laser and Laser Radial.

Danielle, what is your training plan for the 2000 Olympic Trials in the Europe Dinghy?

I sail three days on, one off and another three days on for each cycle. Each daily sailing session is three hours per day and I set daily goals for practice efficiency. I train with training partners so that I can work on my boat speed and test equipment. I work out five days a week in the gym for two hours. On top of that, I stretch every day for a half an hour.

Describe these daily goals. What are some examples?

Daily goals are based on how I feel physically, which point of sail I wish to address, and the type of weather also dictates the day's daily plan. For example, when I train in Hawaii during the summer, I can count on big waves and a strong breeze so I will devote a lot of time to downwind technique. Regardless of the weather, I make sure to have a plan before I hit the water.

How has sailing the Laser or Laser Radial helped you in training in the Europe Dinghy?

I grew up sailing the full rig against the guys. I think that really helped my aggression and motivation. I always sailed in the toughest and hardest Laser or Radial events I could so that I would be pushed to get better. The Laser is a great one-design class where I learned most of my tactics, starts and the importance of fitness in sailing.

What have been your strong points in your success with the Laser Radial?

My fitness, boat handling, and speed have always been very strong in the Radial.

You have raced both the Laser and Laser Radial very successfully. In what ways, if any, do you set up or sail the Radial versus the full rig?

The major difference between the full rig and the Radial is that the radial leech is tighter. This means in the Radial you sheet less and use less vang upwind. I don't recommend two-blocking the Radial rig because the sail will stall and you will park. You also use less vang downwind in the Radial and should adjust the purchase in your vang if you are switching between the two.

Has sailing the Radial changed in the past 5–10 years since you have been racing it?

Internationally I see people using less cunningham and pinching more in light to medium breeze, although I am not sure if this is necessarily faster. I also see more people sailing the Radial and more junior events have shifted from the full rig to the Radial, such as the Cressy (High School Single-handed Championships.)

Did sailing have anything to do with how you met your husband?

John and I met on the Olympic trail for the 1996 Olympics. He was the number-one-ranked Laser sailor in 1995 for the U.S. I was one of the favorites competing in the Europe. Neither of us qualified, but we were married in the summer of 1998 and are actively doing another campaign for the 2000 Games. We practice against each other all the time, switching from the Europe to the full rig. We strike a balance with each other that is important when undertaking a full-time endeavor such as an Olympic campaign. We are both incredibly competitive, but we keep the sport in perspective for each another and we are having fun.

John, you have been competing in world events against the best competition for the past few years. What are the top sailors doing now in terms of adjusting the general sail controls?

As far as the sail controls are concerned, the order of depowering the sail plan is still cunningham first, followed by vang, and then outhaul. Cunningham first, to keep the draft of the sail forward and open the top of the leech to spill power, then the vang to tighten the leech and maintain sail shape while easing the sheet. The outhaul is the very last control to depower because flattening the foot eliminates the foil of the sail and you lose power for punching through waves. The difference now is that everyone is depowering less and less as the fitness level of the sailors increases.

You talk about tightening the cunningham, then vang, and finally the outhaul to depower. How much tightening are you talking about? Also, I assume to power up you reverse the process. When do you start to power up?

The amount of depowering is directly proportional to the size and fitness of the sailor. Those that are not in "Laser shape," and weigh less, are going to have more tension on the cunningham, vang, and outhaul. For some, the cunningham grommet can be pulled down to the boom in extreme breeze ranges. The vang can be maxed out to the point where it becomes necessary to ease it during tacks to clear the boom, then pulled in tight after the tack is complete. You always, even in a survival breeze, want at least 2 to 3 inches of space between the midpoint of the foot of the sail and the middle of the boom when it comes to outhaul. As with any change in velocity, gear shifting becomes necessary, and it is important to react to the decreases in velocity by easing the vang first, so as not to lose pointing ability, and cunningham second to retain power in the upper leech.

What changes have evolved in the past 5–10 years in this area?

Trimming and tuning techniques have remained relatively the same for upwind; however, the top guys are sailing with a much deeper and looser outhaul downwind to maximize power off the wind.

Are there new ideas or techniques that have surfaced for rigging?

Six to one vang systems have become the norm along with the placement of two thimbles in the cunningham and outhaul systems to reduce friction. Within the last half decade, Kevlar became legal for use in all but the vang and hiking strap system. Also, a low profile tiller made of carbon with a 50-inch tiller extension provides greater hiking ability.

Some sailors lead their cunninghams with all parts on the starboard side of the boom while others rig on the port side. Is there an advantage to rigging on one side or the other? And how do you decide how much purchase (mechanical advantage) to use?

Rigging the cunningham to one side provides the ability to pull the cunningham grommet level with or even below the boom, which is favorable in extreme (30 knots and up) wind conditions. However, having the cunningham purchase system all on one side can mean more friction, which makes it more difficult to adjust, especially in a hiking position. Furthermore, pulling the cunningham to one side of the boom produces more draft in the luff of the sail and provides more power on one tack and less on the other, which is fine if you are expecting short steep chop on one tack that will require more power to get through. Having the cunningham set on both sides reduces friction and promotes an even pull on both sides of the sail. However, the differences are nominal and it is a matter of personal preference. As with any sail control, there is no one way of rigging it. The

one question to keep in mind when experimenting with your controls is, does it work for me in every condition?

How about steering? Anything new here? Weight placement/movement, etc.?

Radical body movements both fore and aft along with power hiking and aggressive steering through the waves have elevated today's serious Laser sailor to the status of elite athlete. Droop hiking is a thing of the past, as straight-legging with the shoulders dropped and level with or lower than the deck for extended periods of time is the standard.

Are kinetics a bigger factor in making the boat go fast now than they used to be?

Along with this increase in physical exertion, kinetics plays a major role in boat speed as every wave both upwind and downwind is answered with a body movement to either power through, catch, or avoid each wave.

Like Danielle, you are training for the 2000 Olympic Trials, but in the Laser class. In pursuing this goal, how important is it to have a coach or training partner?

Assistance from a coach or training partner is critical to maximizing your effort. Although I didn't win my trials during my last campaign, I finished fourth and was considered a favorite to win. I attribute my success to the endless hours of work with my training partner. There is only so much a person can accomplish on their own. There are many effective drills that can be done with a partner, not to mention the motivating factor of another person keeping you focused. For this campaign, I am seeking the best people to train with to become time-efficient and effective.

On-the-Water Practicing

ED BAIRD

In the late 1970s, Ed Baird, from St. Petersburg, Florida, consistently finished in the top 10 in major Laser regattas. Most of his finishes were around fourth or fifth, but he found it difficult to move up into the top places. Ultimately, he broke the mold by winning the Midwinter's in two consecutive years, 1980 and 1981, capped by a victory at the largest ever Laser Worlds in Kingston, Ontario, in 1980. Moving out of Lasers, he won the J/24 Worlds in 1983, the International 50-Foot Class Worlds in 1991 and the World Match Racing Championship in 1995. Baird joined America's Cup winner Team New Zealand in 1995 as coach and sparring partner and in 1998 was selected as skipper of *Young America* for the Y2K America's Cup Challenge. Never the type of person who spent time doing road work or lifting weights, Baird attributes a good portion of his success to on-the-water practice. Here he shares his thoughts about how that was undertaken in the Laser, and then on how Laser sailing has helped him in larger boats including becoming the skipper of an America's Cup boat.

Before we start discussing practicing, what was your Laser background leading up to your first Midwinter victory?

I really started sailing the Laser in March 1977. I raced in a few local regattas in South Carolina and Georgia, did pretty well, then went to the Nationals in Fort Lauderdale. There, I had several finishes in the 20s, but because everyone else finished inconsistently, I ended up fifth overall. I think I only had one top-10 finish in that event. After that, I raced a lot of Florida regattas, and while at Florida State, I sailed collegiately. I had three roommates at State who were also Laser sailors, so we practiced a lot together and sailed the Midwinters, Nationals, and whatever else was close enough to drive to.

At what point did you decide you wanted to press on for the Worlds?

In 1977, because of my fifth place at the Nationals, I got an invitation to go to the Worlds in Brazil, but I declined because it was pretty expensive, and I just didn't feel I had sailed Lasers enough to be ready to go to a Worlds. So I stuck around and raced that year's Midwinters, where I got a fifth. Eventually, even though fifth is not bad, I decided I was ready to move up, got real psyched up, and began practicing some of the finer points of Laser sailing to try to improve.

So, you decided there was still quite a bit you could do to pull yourself from fifth up to second or first?

That's right. I realized it was just the little stuff—I was ending up fifth by finishing in the low teens all the time, with maybe a third thrown in here or there. There always seemed to be the group of guys at the very top, and then there were the rest of us. I was always at the top of that second group, and I began to feel that after so long, that was kind of ridiculous. I was not strong, my hiking was poor, and I got tired whenever I was racing. I knew there was a lot more I could do if I got my act together, so I started practicing really hard.

Let's talk about your on-the-water practicing in two sections—what you did when you were alone, and what you did when you had other people out there to practice with.

When I first started sailing the Laser, I mainly tried to learn all of the basic moves. Most of that was done by myself. I just went out and tried to get strong, learn how to hike, learn what happened when I shifted my weight around and all of that sort of thing. I really didn't do any fancy drills or boat handling maneuvers; I just went out to try to get used to the boat. Later, say at the end of 1979 and into 1980, I'd take a marker out and practice rounding that.

Later on, after you had gotten used to the boat, did you go through any specific drills?

I worked on whatever felt good for that day, depending on the breeze and waves. For instance, if it was windy, I'd practice jibes. In light and medium air, if there were waves, I'd practice sailing through them.

When sailing alone, was there anything you tried to avoid so you wouldn't get frustrated or burned out and not want to practice any more?

I tried to analyze how I was doing, not in a judgmental way, but more from a detached point of view. I watched myself as an outsider and said, "Well, am I doing this the way it should be done? Is there any different way I could do it?" It was all kind of an experiment. But basically, by just sailing a lot, I picked up the style that was good for me—the hiking form that was comfortable, the tacking methods that were good.

How did you get yourself strong for hiking?

I can remember going out in the summertime when I was getting ready for a regatta and sailing three miles or so upwind to a marker out in the bay. I spent a lot of time on each tack, hiking as hard as I could. I'd find myself breathing real hard, feeling uncomfortable, and switching positions—trying to do whatever was necessary to stay out there. It's like running four miles if you've never done it before. You really don't know what to expect, and you don't know exactly how to pace yourself, but you just keep trying, and finally you get there. Eventually, after sailing long upwind legs enough, I didn't hurt anymore. By the time the summer of the 1980 Worlds rolled around, I could go sailing without really thinking about my legs hurting, being tired or whatever. I could hike as long as I wanted and concentrate entirely on the race.

What's the optimum situation for practicing with another boat?

A really good situation I've been in is when we've both had the same goal—maybe we were going to the same regatta. Unless there's really something to work for, practicing just doesn't seem as successful. It's also important that both of you be of equal caliber and that neither has a negative attitude. If you don't do well, you know that with some practice you can improve. Another important factor is that each person be able to share what you do and learn. We would talk with each other all the time, exchanging information about how we were doing and what we thought the other person was doing right or wrong.

How about when you're out there sailing with that person; is there anything you should avoid?

Try to stay away from trying real hard just to beat the other person, tactically. What you want to work on is speed and boat handling, not something like pinching someone off or sailing down over them. For working on boat speed, each boat has to have clear air and room to breathe, so make sure you both understand that. You're trying to sail faster than the other person, but not be abusive about it.

What kind of specific drills do you recommend when practicing with someone else?

We came up with a tacking and jibing game to help those maneuvers. In the tacking game, we basically tried to cover the guy behind, and the guy behind would try to pass the boat ahead. For jibing, the guy behind would always try to jibe inside the guy ahead and get on his air. The two games are very similar in that they both involve one boat trying to pass the other by jibing or tacking more efficiently and quickly.

How did you work on starting?

A lot of times, my roommates and I, plus some other people in the area, would go out sailing each evening after work. We usually ended up with three to five boats, and we'd go out, set up a short course with a 2- to 3-minute weather leg, and just race a lot. That was really good for learning how to position yourself at the start properly and how to keep people out of your way at the start. We'd count down from 60 to 0 and then start. Between 4 P.M. and when we'd quit, about 7:30 P.M., we'd sail maybe 10 to 20 short races. Pretty soon, it didn't matter how you did in each race, because you'd forget about that race after two or three more. So you just tried your best all the time, experimenting with different starting techniques each race. It was especially challenging because we were all about the same caliber.

Did your practicing in any way affect your attitude going into the 1980 Worlds?

I had practiced awhile that summer, but then I sailed in some regattas that I did poorly in just before the Worlds. So I really didn't go into the event expecting to win. I knew I would do fairly well because of what practicing I had done, but because of those recent poor finishes, I decided I'd just try to do the best I could.

Do you think that attitude helped you?

Yes. I do that all the time now, as a matter of fact. If you have too much to prove, you get into the dangerous situation of getting real nervous about how you're doing. But if you don't have anything to lose, you can approach it with a much cooler attitude. If you go just to see how you'll do, just to enjoy the sport, I think you'll get a lot more out of it, and you'll probably do better.

Fast forward to the year 2000. Now that you have moved on to bigger boats, match racing, and America's Cup fame, what lessons learned in Laser sailing have you taken with you?

Years of racing the Laser gave me the skills to feel and understand wind and water, and to get a boat through them efficiently. In America's Cup boats, and other big race boats where I have access to large amounts of performance data from the instruments, feel and an intuitive sense of what the boat needs is still vital. The numbers can only tell you so much. In the end, it's up to me to know if the boat is going well. The Laser also taught me how to manage risk on the race course. Now I work in the complicated environment of 16 crew and millions of dollars of sophisticated equipment, but the basics are still the same. Know what your exposure is, and choose the best option for improving your position. Whether I'm on the line in a 100-boat fleet, or match racing on the Auckland harbor, my time in the Laser gave me the skills to win anywhere.

A Heavyweight's Guide to Light Air Sailing

TOM LIHAN

Tom Lihan had extensive experience and success in the Laser during the 1980s. As a heavyweight, he sailed at between 185 to 195 pounds, which was considered on the heavy side for Lasers in the era prior to 3.8-ounce sails. He won many of his events in light to medium winds, including the 1982 North Americans, Collegiate Single-Handed Championship, and the O'Day Trophy for the Men's Single-Handed Championship. He won the Finn North Americans in 1983 and the Finn Midwinters in 1994. Tom reentered the Laser class in 1995, winning the U.S. trials for the Pan Am Games held in Mar del Plata, Argentina. At 195 to 200 pounds, Tom is still on the heavy side, yet some of his most successful regattas have been in light to medium winds. Here he shares some of his ideas for getting the most out of the Laser in those conditions.

Despite your weight, you have always managed to do well in light and medium winds. In such a weight-oriented boat, how do you explain that?

I do enjoy sailing in light and medium airs and have been happy with my success in those conditions. I certainly didn't have a lot of boat speed in less than 10 knots, but since variations in breeze direction and velocity are much more important, light air sailing becomes more of a tactical event than sailing in moderate and heavy conditions. In medium winds—between 12 and 16 knots—everyone's speed is very close. There also aren't a lot of major wind shifts. So, even with my weight, in those conditions everyone is pretty equal. Good basics—starts, corners, and clear lanes—count a lot in medium air. But with less than 10 knots of wind, you start getting a lot of major wind shifts, and smart sailing often pays off more than boat speed. If you get big 30-degree wind shifts, you can gain and lose very quickly; it's much more tactical than any other condition. You find yourself standing up in the boat looking a quarter-mile to windward for the wind. You really need to be aware of what is going on.

In light air, one of the most difficult legs of the course for heavier sailors always seems to be off-wind. Do you find yourself losing what you gained on the upwind legs whenever you go downhill?

As a matter of fact, I do pretty well offwind in light air, and I think it's largely due to concentration. I have taken techniques learned in the Laser and applied them to other classes as well as big boats—simply sail in a clear lane headed towards the next puff and never stop concentrating on boat speed. I always used to look astern for other boats that might be gaining on me, but quickly learned that you need to use all your brainpower to perform well in constantly changing conditions. If there are waves, I watch them, always trying to position the boat correctly relative to them. As long as I am playing them 100 percent, I'll be difficult to catch. I also watch sail trim. That's a critical point in light air. Let the mainsheet out just 6 inches, and it can make a big difference, particularly in waves. What happens is the apparent wind is changing so quickly that you've got to keep the sheet moving—easing it out a bit whenever you slow down and trimming it back in whenever you speed up. Of course, it's also being continually adjusted for any course changes. The theories behind sailing a Laser downhill in light air are magnified in boats such as Melges 24s and Scows, where a 2-knot velocity increase allows you to sail deeper and faster; a 2-knot velocity increase with a 5-degree header can mean instant gains to the front of the fleet. The same techniques apply to a Laser, but it's much more difficult to feel and see the results due to the slower speed and less rapid acceleration.

What kinds of things do you watch for in the sail that tell you when to trim or ease it?

In the Laser it's all feel in the mainsheet and the hiking stick. I use the same mainsheet all the time so that I know exactly what that feel is going to be like (¼-inch Marstron). I do have a couple of ribbons on the sail. I like those better than yarns because I can hear them ticking against the sail when they are not flowing smoothly. So I actually end up listening to them more than looking at them. Using too much helm in light air also acts as much more of a brake than in a breeze. Two-finger steering and body weight adjustments are much more efficient. My coach at Kings Point, Ken Legler, used to make us sail entire practices in Lasers and 420s without tillers; I seem to recall that I was very good at that drill.

Do you adjust your vang much offwind?

In the early days of Lasers, we only had 3:1 vangs. The popular style of upwind sailing in moderate to heavy air was to sit on the boom before the start, set the vang cleat, and forget about it until the end of the race. Likewise in light air, the vang was set upwind in order to prebend the mast and take enough draft out of the middle front so you could point uphill. No one thought to let the vang off downhill. Then about 1980, I was really getting killed offwind by the Canadians—Terry Nielson, Greg Tawaststjerna, and Steve Fleckenstein especially. So I said, "What are you guys doing downwind?" They said, "Do you let your vang off?" and I said, "Not at all." And that was the problem. So then we had to learn how to put a 3:1 vang on at the bottom mark in both light and heavy air, the latter being much more difficult. The range I would ease it is only about 2 inches—just enough so that the mast comes very close to being straight without allowing the luff of the sail to get too round. It

might have 2 or 3 inches of bend at most. If you let it off beyond that, totally straightening the mast, you lose some luff curve. That luff curve is cut into the sail, and if the mast is not bent a little, that luff curve will be pulled out, and you lose sail area. Then, after I had left the class circuit for a few years in the middle 1980s, this tall skinny kid named Brett Davis came back from one of the World youth regattas and showed us what the New Zealanders and Australians were doing with purchases on the vang. Today, of course, adjustment is not a logistical issue but more of a tuning device. The same theory applies however, and I've watched Robert Scheidt's stern disappear in 25 knots after easing the vang substantially after rounding the top mark. In light air, a bit of McLube will allow the multipurchase to work, and the top sailors are setting the vangs similar to what we discovered back around 1980.

Do you make many modifications to your boat, or do you sail it pretty much stock from the factory?

Today's Lasers are superior to the boats turned out before 1992. Prior to that, most of the builders were allowing large variations in hull and deck weight, mast rake, hull stiffness, and fairness. In the past, several of us had reputations for spending time working on Lasers and searching for the optimal hull and spar set. Today, the most important thing is for the boat not to leak or break. Stock boats are used "as is" by almost all the top sailors since so many regattas are at international venues offering quality charter boats. The builders have recognized their weaknesses and corrected them. I remember discussions with Peter Johnstone in which I showed him my spreadsheet of mast rakes indicating over a 4-inch range at the top of the mast. He implemented a jig system which I believe is now standard. The only real modifications are in lines and rigging as well as a sailor's personal-style tiller.

You have sailed Finns, Snipes, Melges 24s, and Farr 40s a lot. How do they compare to the Laser?

In all the other one-design classes that I have sailed, the most important lesson I have learned from the Laser is that even using identical boats, top sailors have the ability to outperform "tail-enders" by huge margins. Consider the fact that at the Laser Worlds, the winner of a race usually finishes at least a leg or more ahead of the middle of the fleet. This advantage is due simply to sailing faster and in the right direction. There are no rating advantages, no sailmaker advantages, no hull shape variations, just plain basic better sailing. Now then, think about the other variables which can occur in classes such as the Melges 24 (kite and sail design), the Finn (mast/sail combo), Farr 40 (rig tune, jib choice), or Snipe (hull shape and crew weight), and try to imagine all the excuses that a skipper could think of other than his or her sailing ability! I have learned very well that you must first look at the variables which sailors create by their tactics, sail trim, or steering before fooling around with a boat which is probably pretty well set up to begin with. At the top level in most one-design classes, all the "first-row" competitors are pretty much using the same equipment so one can't blame the boat. As I've grown older, I always remember the Laser events I have participated in, the mistakes made, and think of how great a variable the actual driver or tactician is in the whole equation of winning sailboat races. The Laser teaches you to concentrate on the basics when racing rather than look to your equipment or boat for performance excuses. I have not met any sailors in my life who have been able to win major events simply because their raw boat speed was superior. A lot of PHRF (Performance Handicap Racing Factor) and big boat sailors who have never raced Lasers or other strict performance one-designs do not comprehend where their faults and improvement areas lie.

How much do you move around in the boat off-wind, especially fore and aft?

In light air, a heavy person like myself can very easily put the bow or the stern in the water too far, and that will really stop you. So you have to be careful about your fore-and-aft movements.

If I'm concerned about the range of my movements, I usually glance back over the stern and see if my waves are catching up with the rudder. If they are, I'm too far aft. As far as the actual distance I move is concerned, it naturally increases as the wind picks up. But for a benchmark figure, at about 12 knots, I might be moving fore and aft as much as 18 inches in waves. Of course in a big breeze and waves, the athleticism required to sail downwind is almost more than that required to sail upwind. The range of motion is extreme by older standards, and today's top sailors have made the biggest improvement gains in offwind speed and technique.

Are you always going for a neutral helm?

Yes, it's all done by steering with my weight. I used to practice by sailing without a tiller, which forced me to get used to sailing that way. And that's really important in the Laser. Any time the rudder is turned with tiller force, that same amount of effort is being translated into a braking effect on boat speed as the rudder is turned against the natural flow of water. In light air, since you do not have very much horsepower available, you want to be extremely careful not to induce unnecessary drag.

Obviously you have the cunningham eased off-wind in light air, but what about the outhaul?

In the old days, we would ease it off a bit, but not that much. If you let it out too far, it was always difficult to bring back on as you went upwind. Today, with the purchase system, adjustments are much easier to accomplish. There is a point however, when you create too full a sail, and the air flow gets detached too quickly. When I was at school we did some research on that, and we read Marchaj's book on aerodynamics, *Sailing Theory and Practice*. It all told us the same thing: in light air, a sail that was too full was just not as effective as a sail that was slightly flatter. So as it gets lighter, I often tension the outhaul a bit.

Upwind, how do you maintain boat speed when there are no major shifts to keep you up front?

As when sailing downhill in light air, the most important thing I do for my boat speed upwind is to keep sailing in clear lanes. Turbulence or wind shadows in light air are much more of a factor than in a breeze. Tacking in light to medium air can also be more painful than in 12–15 knots (not to be confused with roll tacking in 0–5 knots). As in the earlier days of Laser sailing, today it's important not to use too much cunningham tension in anything under 15 knots. I get a lot of wrinkles from the middle of the luff back to the clew, and with the 3.8-ounce sail, the draft stays right where it was designed. In any-thing over 12 knots, or when you are in the straps, the cunningham begins to come on before the outhaul. This is the single biggest difference between the old days, with soft 3.2-ounce sails, and today. From a leverage or physics stand-point, it makes much more sense to dump horse-power in the top of the sail than in the bottom. For this reason, the cunningham, which pulls the draft forward and opens the leech from the numbers up, should be the first depower gear to pull. It is now very common to have the cunningham bottomed out and the outhaul set at 4 inches from the boom in 25 knots upwind.

Changing with the Conditions—A World Champion's Perspective

Terry Neilson

One of the most consistent top Laser sailors in the early years was Canadian Terry Neilson, who placed seventh at the 1979 Worlds in Australia, ninth at the 1980 Worlds in Kingston, and won the 1982 Worlds in Sardinia. His other Laser victories include three Canadian championships, the Europeans, the Pan American Games, and finishes in the top three places at the U.S. Nationals and U.S. Midwinters. One key to his many wins was his ability to shift gears—change the way his boat was set up and the way he sailed it—as conditions changed, thus allowing him to sail the boat at its optimum performance level all the time. Here, he explains some of his techniques and the ideas behind them.

Many racers talk about the ability to shift gears in the Laser, and it seems the ability to do that quickly and accurately often means the difference between a good Laser sailor and a great one. When you think of shifting gears in the Laser, what comes to mind?

Let's say I'm going from heavy to medium wind in a race; in other words, the wind is dying. Before, I was overpowered, but now I suddenly find myself with not enough power to push through the waves the way I was doing earlier. As soon as I recognize that, I begin to make ad-justments in the three main controls—the out-haul, cunningham, and boom vang—in order to generate as much power as I can possibly han-dle. I also begin moving a little differently in the boat, for as the wind lightens, you can usu-ally torque the boat over the waves much more easily, which means using the tiller less, thus making the boat go faster.

So, you are basically making changes in two categories—sail controls and body movement. Could you explain the control adjustments first, taking them one at a time?

Sure. Many people make the mistake of setting the cunningham too tight. You should never touch the cunningham, leaving it completely slack, until you're overpowered, meaning you can no longer hold the boat perfectly flat. There will be some wrinkles along the luff, and if they're extreme, just reach up and tug down on the sail tack with your hand.

What's the advantage of carrying the cunningham that loose for so long?

The cunningham affects leech tension and the sail entry. Tighten the cunningham and you open up the leech, reducing the fineness of the sail entry. Opening the leech takes away power, and reducing a fine sail entry hinders pointing ability.

Where do you go with the cunningham tension once overpowered?

Gradually begin trimming until you're back in control. If you've been spending a fair amount of time in the boat, you should be able to feel the difference as you crank it down. You want just enough cunningham tension to allow you to hold the boat flat. If you're shifting gears in a dramatically increasing wind, you may need to pull the cunningham all the way in, which means tightening it until the cunningham grommet is right on top of the boom.

At the same time, would you be shifting gears with the outhaul?

Well, the outhaul only affects the bottom 20 or 30 percent of the sail. The more you ease it, the more power you generate in that section of the sail. However, even when it's windy, that power doesn't hurt you much because it's so low that it's not creating much heeling moment. It can affect the leech a bit, tightening it as you ease the outhaul, but that only happens if you let it off quite a bit.

So, that means you generally carry the outhaul quite loose?

The majority of the time, the middle of the sail foot is 6 to 8 inches off the boom, unless it's re-

ally howling. Then, I'll carry it 2 to 3 inches off the boom. The only time I'll carry it looser than 6 to 8 inches is when the wind is dying but there are still some waves. Then, I need all the power I can get to move through them. I might carry it as much as 10 inches off the boom.

What do you look for in the sail when you're adjusting the vang to changing conditions?

I really don't look at the sail that much. What I will look at is the angle of the mainsheet at the stern. When I let the mainsheet out, I watch how far the boom goes up before it starts going just sideways.

What are your vang tension benchmarks for each condition?

Generally, the windier it is, the more vang I put on. I think of vang adjustment in a couple of different positions. If the vang is loose, the boom will go up 12 to 18 inches before beginning to go just sideways. The other extreme is really tight, which means it will only go up about 2 inches before just moving sideways. It usually takes about 5 or 10 minutes of upwind sailing to tell where to set it. I hike full out, and if I'm overpowered, I put on more vang. If my butt is starting to drag in the water, I ease the vang a little bit. I'm always setting the vang to give me as much power as I can possibly handle.

Do you use any reference points on the vang line?

Yes, I put a mark on the middle strand, which becomes my stationary point of reference, then I put three marks on the forward-most line. The middle mark represents block-to-block vanging. To determine that position, I sheet the mainsheet block-to-block, then just take up the slack in the vang. The bottom mark indicates the super-vanging position. To set that, I pull the main in until it is block-to-block and cleat it off. Then, I reach forward and take the slack out of the vang. The highest mark is for light winds and reaches in winds of around 10 knots. I sheet the main so the stern blocks are 2 to 3 inches apart and take up the vang slack.

So, how far would it be from the top mark to the bottom mark on that forward strand of vang line?

Probably around 3 inches at most. Remember, the vang is a very finicky control, and when it gets windy, it's probably the most critical adjustment on the boat. Although I have three spots marked off, it gets adjusted a lot in between.

It's clear how the vang, cunningham, and outhaul help you gain or lose power as you shift gears for the conditions, but how does body movement fit into changing gears?

Using your body when shifting gears is largely a factor of the water conditions. The idea is to always keep the waterline as long as possible, because that's what makes you go faster. In smooth water, that means sitting as far forward in the cockpit as you can. Some people think it helps to get further forward, but you only end up in a very uncomfortable position, usually on your back looking straight up. That may make you go a bit faster, but you probably will not have a clue about what's going on around you. Once you start getting into waves, you must move aft. What tells me to move aft is that I will start taking waves over the bow, say, one in every ten waves. If I'm not taking any waves at all over the bow, then I'm probably sitting too far aft.

How about fore-and-aft movement of your upper body?

Again, it's a function of increasing the waterline whenever possible. It's tough for fore-and-aft upper body movement to have much of an effect in heavy air, but once you get to the point where you can start torquing the boat around some, it can really pay off. What I try to avoid doing is plowing into a wave. So, as I'm coming into the crest of a wave, I lean aft, allowing the bow to lift a little easier. Once on top of the wave, I lean forward to keep the bow down and to keep the boat's full length in the water.

What kind of tiller movements would you be making in conjunction with those movements?

If I'm moving my upper body fore and aft a lot, I will also be moving my tiller. My tiller ends at the aft end of the cockpit, and in wavy conditions I would probably be moving it a total of 12 to 18 inches, sometimes going down and back up in just a second or so. What I'm doing with it is playing each wave, if they're big enough. As I get just past the trough and am almost to the crest, I stick the tiller to leeward and lean my upper body aft. Then, as I go over the top of the wave, I pull the tiller up and lean forward to get the boat fully back in the water. If the waves are smaller, I might do this on only every fifth wave or so. In flat water, I move the tiller as little as possible. Then, I steer using my upper body to heel the boat slightly to leeward to head up and slightly to windward to bear off. Probably the place I steer the most is in 10 to 15 knots of wind and heavy chop. When it gets much windier than that, I have enough power in the sail to drive through the waves, and hiking keeps me going well.

Are you also playing your main in choppy conditions?

There are only two conditions where I really play the main. That's in light wind, under 5 or 6 knots, and in choppy conditions when I get hit by a gust that overpowers me. In light wind, I am constantly trying to find the optimum range of mainsheet trim. That's usually just a matter of feel and watching the sail ribbons. The faster I go, the more I pull the mainsheet in. When I start to slow down, I let it off a little bit until my speed builds back up. The same is true in waves, when the wind is light. As soon as I hit a wave and slow down, I let the main off a bit to get going again. If I trim it too soon, there won't be enough power in the sail, as it will be too flat and will stall out. When it's windy, above 15 knots, I usually don't play the main unless I get overpowered. Then, I will dump the main off maybe as much as a foot.

But that's only if I find myself in a situation where I can't keep the boat flat by feathering it.

As you're sailing upwind, are you also watching the sail?

If I've been sailing for two or three months, I can usually sail just by feel, except in light winds when I watch the sail ribbons. For those who can't spend that much time in the boat, the ribbons are the best all-around guide.

Are you trying to keep both windward and leeward ribbons flowing smoothly aft all the time?

It's more a matter of determining what is optimally close-hauled for your sail and the way you have the boat set up. The best way to check that is in flat water. Head up slowly until the luff of the sail—right behind the mast and about a foot up from the boom—just starts to luff. You're watching for about a centimeter of movement. At that point, look up at your sail ribbons and note how they're flowing. That's where you want the ribbons to be whenever you're sailing upwind. If you're fairly new to it, you might crank off just a touch and note where the ribbons are at that point. That will provide a slightly more forgiving close-hauled course.

Any final suggestions for keeping the boat moving well in changing conditions?

Keep the boat flat. Everyone tells you that, but few listen. It took a long time before I did. You can go out with about 90 percent of the Laser sailors, and if you look at them and say, "Sail the boat flat," they will respond, "I am." But they're still heeling 5 or 10 degrees. Then, you tell them to keep flattening it out, more and more. When the boat's finally flat, they will say, "No, I'm heeling to windward." So, good advice would be always to sail so you feel as if you're heeling to windward, then you'll know the boat is flat.

Preparing Physically to Win a Major Championship

JOHN BERTRAND

The first person to win the Laser World Championship a second time was San Francisco's John Bertrand, winning at Kiel, Germany, in 1976 and Cabo Frio, Brazil, in 1977. For Bertrand, winning in 1976 did not mean an easy shot at the title again the next year. Rather, it indicated many new areas to focus on during the interim.

Going into the 1977 Laser Worlds in Brazil, knowing that it was going to be a rather windy series, did you do anything different in preparation than in 1976?

After the Laser Worlds in 1976, I was very disappointed as far as how I was physically and technically in the boat.

Even though you won the regatta?

Yes. Tactically, I sailed very well, but physically and technically, just tacking and jibing, I was not in very good shape. So, it became my goal to do something physically about that. I could see the direct relationship of fitness converted into boat speed. So, for the next year leading up to the 1977 Worlds, I went into a heavy training program, which consisted of running five days a week, 5 to 6 miles, usually integrating hill work every other day for endurance. I started to take modern dance and worked my way up to nine 1½-hour classes a week. That was for increased flexibility and better control over movement and better overall body control. I also lifted weights 3 days a week.

Did you do any specific types of weight training?

Not really. I just worked on overall conditioning. I never got into the really heavy weightlifting program where I balloon up or anything like that. I was lifting more for speed and endurance—lighter weights with more repetitions.

You knew you would probably be wearing a weight jacket in Brazil. Did you do any particular exercises to prepare for that?

Obviously, stomach and back strength was really important. There was one exercise I did for that in the weight room, and I'm positive it helped me. It's sort of a bench that you sit on, and you can hook your legs under it. There are two ways you can do the exercise. You can lie face down and bend over 90 degrees to the floor, then arch your back up. You can either put a weight behind your head or hold your hands up at your head. Those are like back extensions, where you start with your head down at the floor (your upper body 90 degrees to the floor), then arch as high as possible, if you can even get above level. I would usually do about 15 of those or as many as it took for me to fatigue. Your muscles aren't very strong back there, so it's easy to tire quickly. Then, I'd flip over and bend down so my head was almost to the floor and pull myself up again. I've talked to many people since then who say that puts an awful lot of stress on your lower back. So, I worked my way into those very slowly. I ended up doing about 20 or 30 each session, which would be enough to really fatigue me. It was hard enough as it was, so I never did it with weights.

What other exercises did you do in preparation for the Worlds?

Before every workout, I would do about 75 to 100 sit-ups, and afterward I would do about the same. The proper way to do sit-ups is really important. When you start, in the sitting position, the proper way to go back is to roll down your spine, rather than having your spine fairly flat and sort of falling back. What you do is tuck your chin in and then concentrate on keeping your spine pinned to the floor. When you roll up, you concentrate on doing the same thing, instead of bouncing up. Your back fatigues much earlier than your stomach muscles. If you have very strong stomach muscles and weak back muscles, that right there makes you very susceptible to back injuries. This sit-up method also keeps the muscles tense through the whole movement. Of course, never do sit-ups with your legs straight, as that puts a lot of pressure on your lower back. Always have them bent. The steeper you bend them, the harder the exercise will be.

What sort of practice did you do to improve your technical ability in the boat, such as tacking and jibing?

I spent a lot of time tacking and jibing, and going through a lot of drills. I discovered that it was much easier to practice if you broke everything down into smaller parts rather than taking a look at the big picture. I'd break down everything required to be successful in a race rather than focusing on everything at once. For instance, I'd work on starts by going through a "stop-and-go" drill. The idea was to totally stop the boat, then try to accelerate as fast as possible.

Did you spend a lot of time simply sailing the boat?

At the height of my training, I maybe sailed five days a week for around two hours a day. I discovered that if I stayed out on the water too long, I would begin to get stale. A couple of hours was just enough to keep me anxious about getting out the next time. Plus, I knew a lot of people who spent a lot of time in the boat, got stale and wouldn't sail for weeks at a time. I would always go out, even if it was only for 20 minutes or so, just time enough to practice a few tacks, then head in. So, during the course of the summer, I probably totaled more actual sailing time than the others did.

Do you have any philosophies about how a practice session should be approached?

Always push yourself slightly above your limit. When you just feel comfortable, don't stop; just keep working on it until you feel like you'll drop dead. Then rest a bit and practice some more. I also found it was important to focus on my weak points. It's always very easy to work on your strengths because that's usually very satisfying. The tendency is to overlook your weak points because they're tougher to work on.

What weak points did you feel you had to focus on?

The biggest one was the boat's toughest point of sail, which is a very close reach. There, the Laser tends to want to tip over, and you have to hike very hard to hold it flat. That takes a lot of stamina. Realizing that a very close reach does not occur very often in Laser races, I practiced it anyway, just in case it might arise. And in Brazil, it did. The first reaches tended to be almost runs, which made the second reaches very

tight. But I had trained for that point of sail, knowing how tough it was and that it was a specific weakness, and I was able to take advantage of the situation. I also spent a lot of time training for light air, even though I knew the regatta was going to be windy. And sure enough, it turned out the first two races were light, and my practice paid off.

What would you say is the most critical phase of Laser racing?

If someone had only a limited amount of time to put into practicing, I would say work on your starts. My starts at the Worlds in Brazil were mostly middle-of-the-line, but because of other practice, I was able to climb back up through the fleet, if necessary. Most of the time, I rounded the first weather mark in the top 20, and later in the regatta, as people began to fatigue, I was usually in the top 10. Once I was even 48th, but a 30-degree wind shift later on in that race still allowed me to win it. I guess what is important about starts is that, from the middle and back of the fleet, you have more obstacles to overcome than if you're in front. If you win the start, everything becomes much simpler.

A Female Perspective

LAINIE PARDEY

Lainie Pardey is one of the most active sailors in the Laser class and has been vice president of the International Laser Class for the North American Region since 1997. She also regularly races the Laser Radial which was named by the International Sailing Federation as an International Class in 1999. From 1996–98 she was ranked first woman on the North American Grand Prix Race Series, which, for Laser class members in North America, awards points based on participation and finishing placement in Class-sanctioned events. Last year more than 600 sailors posted scores. She and her husband, Marsh, tow their Lasers an average of 10,000 miles each year to sail in North American regattas. These are her insights on women sailing Lasers.

What is it that attracts a female sailor to the Laser as compared, for example, with the Finn or Europe Dinghy?

The best thing about Lasers, for women or men, is that you can find them everywhere. No matter how small a place is or how far from a coastline, there are Lasers in people's garages, sailors lurking, and wind and water beckoning a race. There *are* better boats for women to sail, however. The Laser, even with the Radial rig, is a bit overpowered and very physical for the average woman to race competitively. The Europe Dinghy is better suited to women if you just want a single-handed boat to sail. But you just can't find a fleet of Europes to race unless you live in Florida or California. They are also quite expensive and fragile. Lasers, on the other hand, are widely available in a range of prices so most women can find one they can afford. Lasers are also durable and easily repaired and upgraded, which cannot be said of Europes. Very few women can handle the weight and power of a Finn; launching and rigging one is a big job for most men.

What advice would you give a female sailor who has never sailed a Laser but wants to become a competitor?

I'd first advise her to get into shape and stay that way if she wants to compete in Lasers. Strengthen arms, shoulders, and hands, and work on the abs and leg strength. If she's under 140 pounds, I'd advise her to get a Radial rig if there are others racing this rig locally. I'd then advise her to go sailing with a group of Laser sailors who will help her and coach her in the idiosyncrasies of the boat. Starting out, it's easy to get frustrated. A clinic such as the those held by Rick and Mary White or Kolius Sailing in Florida are an ideal starting point. I'd tell her to expect to flip the boat a lot at first and to practice dumping and righting the boat on a light wind day, where the water is warm. That way, if—or more realistically, when—a capsize happens in a race, she won't have to lose a lot of time struggling with the boat and often won't even get wet.

Are there advantages or disadvantages for the female sailor in this boat?

The only advantage I can think of to being female and sailing Lasers is that there are so few females sailing the boat, you are sure to meet lots of great guys at regattas! Less height and lighter weight than the average male and less upper body strength are disadvantages for women competing in Lasers. But there are some tall, very fit women who are excellent Laser sailors. The optimum size and weight for a Laser sailor is 6'1" to 6'2" and around 180 pounds. That's been made clear in recent World Championships and Olympic competition. Very few women this size sail Lasers, but there is still a lot of interest in sailing this boat, particularly with the Radial rig.

Do you envision any changes to the racing rules that should be made to level the playing field for female sailors?

Absolutely not. Sailing is one sport that actually starts with a pretty level playing field because we can choose which boat to sail. Some clubs have included in their sailing instructions that female and master sailors in Lasers are allowed to change rigs from the full rig to the Radial, but only for local club events.

You keep referring to the Laser Radial; is that a better choice for women sailors? What effect will gaining International status have on the Radial?

The Radial, with a 20 percent smaller sail on a shorter mast, is a better rig for women, but it is more difficult to find competitors to race against. If the rule change passes to allow the soft top section and flatter cut sail, it will be even more attractive to women because it will be easier to depower than it is now. The ILCA applied for separate International Status for the Radial because last year ISAF placed limitations on the number of World Championship titles each International Class could award. We would not have been able to give Worlds titles to Open, Youth, Female and Master sailors in both Laser and Radial without separate International status.

Now, with your ILCA Executive Committee hat on, and recognizing that the Laser has basically

maintained its one-design nature since it first came out in 1970, do you feel that changes should be allowed and, if so, how does the class decide which changes would be good for Laser class racing and Laser sailing?

I am absolutely in favor of making carefully considered and researched changes to the Laser. The Laser Class World Council members like to think of the process of changing and improving the Laser as an evolution. Over the years there have been almost 40 changes written into the class rules. None of them have been earth-shattering, or in my opinion have compromised the one-design nature of the Laser. You can still dig a 20-year-old Laser out of somebody's garage and, with some sanding and polishing work and investment in new gear, such as lines and maybe a sail, go out and have a ball racing it. The basic pieces—hulls, spars, and blades—of the Laser are durable, and well standardized.

The process for making a change to the Laser Class Rules is long and rather arduous, which pretty well meshes with our intention of making changes to the boat slowly. It goes like this: A member or group will suggest to one of the class officers a change to the rules that they would like to see. The idea will be presented through the system to the World Council, debated, and if approved, may need to be researched by the builders. Research will start after this World Council meeting, and hopefully be finished by the next one. Since the World Council meets less than once per year, at the World Championship regattas, already 18 months to 2 years may pass before we decide to propose the change. If the research and extensive testing produces a viable design that is inexpensive, and doesn't require a complicated retrofit to the boat, or compromise any structural part of the basic boat, the World Council will then vote

to present the proposal to the members. The proposal is presented in writing to the members in the next issue of *LaserWorld*, the quarterly international newsletter of the class, along with a ballot. Members must fill in and return the ballots by mail or fax within six months of the presentation of the proposal. Any proposal must pass with a two-thirds majority approval of those members who voted. If a proposal is passed by the members, the class must then get approval of ISAF's One-Design council because the Laser is an International and Olympic class. ISAF only meets once every six months, so again this may delay the new rule from coming into effect. Once we have approval of the World Council, the members and the ISAF, we can make the rule change, *but* we are further restricted by the ISAF from making any rule changes within a year before an Olympic event. You can see that it can take three or four years from the conception of a rule change to when it may actually become legal.

As to what kind of changes we should make and their impact upon class racing and Laser sailing, we start by asking, is it going to be expensive? We try to limit the amount anyone can spend on new equipment for their Lasers to prevent people from trying to buy performance. Is it going to involve a complicated retrofit for old boats? By complicated we mean having to do stuff to install the new gadget that your average Laser sailor can't or doesn't want to do themselves. Is it going to compromise any structural part of the basic boat, rig or blades? Sometimes when you make something stronger, a weaker part of the boat may break. Is it going to affect the performance of the boat significantly?

If the answer to any of the above is yes, we don't even consider the rule change proposal. This rule change procedure has helped to maintain the one-design nature of the class.

DAVE OLSON

Dave Olson started sailing Lasers in 1981. He won the 1985 World Masters Games. He was also the 1988 Laser United States Masters Class Champion, and the 1989 Laser North American Overall and Masters Class Champion. In 1990, he won the International Sunfish Masters Championship. He is the proud wearer of the "Green Blazer," having won the 1986 and 1990 Florida Masters Laser Championship. He sails with his wife, Ursula, and his children, Kristina and Jeffery, out of Sarasota, Florida.

Masters Sailing

What's the story behind Masters sailing? How did it get started?

Masters sailing has continued to develop throughout the world over the last decade, particularly in the Laser class. It is not uncommon for 120 to 150 competitors from 20 to 30 countries to attend a Masters Laser World Championship. There are national championships in almost every country where the Laser class is organized, and Masters trophies are given in almost every regional and district Laser regatta.

The origins of Masters sailing are obscure. According to legend, Laser Masters sailing originated in North America when a group in Washington state hosted a regatta for the "over 30s" in 1978. Jeff Martin and the then European Secretary, Jan Romme, formalized the idea, and by 1980 there was enough interest to generate the first Masters Laser World Championship in Bandol, France. The event attracted 67 entries from 14 countries. Since then, there have been Masters World Championships in Australia, New Zealand, Thailand, Europe, North America, South Africa, South America, and Japan. Every four years the Laser is used for the sailing event in the World Masters Games, and this substitutes for the usual world championship. Peter Seidenberg, Jack Swenson, Jim Christopher, and Bob Saltmarsh formed an ad hoc committee to guide the Masters regatta scheduling in North America. The first North American Masters Championship was at the Fort Worth Boat Club in Texas, in 1979. The Canadian Championships, which have become quite popular, started in 1986 in Gimli, Canada. The U.S. Masters Championships began in 1987 at the New Bedford Yacht Club in Massachusetts. The Royal Turkey Yacht Club in North Palm Beach, Florida, hosts the Florida Masters Championship, a prelude to the Midwinters East Regatta when it is held in Florida. Over the past few years regional Masters regattas have sprung up both here and abroad.

What are the differences in Masters sailing?

Masters sailing has evolved from the needs and demands of older sailors in the class. The scoring is set up on a handicap system based on age groups. The classes include Apprentice (35–45 years), Master (45–55 years), Grand Master (55–65 years), and Great Grand Master (over 65 years). To compensate for the age differences in the overall scoring, the two younger divisions are handicapped by adding one point to the score of the Masters and two to the score of the Apprentices. The Great Grand Masters get to subtract a point from their scores. The Grand Masters are exempt from the additional points. This system has worked very well over the years.

But it is not just the scoring that makes Masters racing different from other Laser regattas. A different atmosphere and philosophy is present at Masters regattas. The words *congeniality* and *fraternity* come to mind. When you go to a Masters regatta you sense an almost subliminal understanding that everyone has been busy fulfilling countless responsibilities, and now they are coming together to have some good clean fun in order to rejuvenate the body and spirit. You see friendships refortified, newcomers introduced around, people helped with their boats and equipment—everything moves smoothly. On the water things get serious. It is very competitive sailing. The competitors' accomplishments are appreciated, and their misfortunes are met with empathy. Coming off the water after a hard day of sailing, you get plenty of help on the beach from fellow competitors. Post-race analysis is lively and boisterous. Protests are few, since most rule infractions are handled through on-the-water penalties. Differences which *have* reached the protest room have not been frivolous and are the source of much discussion. Conviviality develops so that all participants have a good time and, despite the adverse circumstances and conditions that can occasionally develop at any regatta, they leave with a warm, comfortable feeling of fatigue of the body and a quiet renewal of the soul.

What is the level of competition in Masters sailing?

I think it is the constraints of time, job, family, and other responsibilities that make it difficult to train and practice to the extent that the younger sailors do. Also, as we get older, we must work more diligently and more carefully to develop and maintain the physical conditioning necessary for competitive sailing. I personally think that these demands on our time decrease the level of performance by approximately 5 to 15 percent when compared, say, to a competitor who is preparing for an Olympic berth.

Do you think that Master sailors can really be successful in the top echelons of Laser competition?

Yes! Studies have indicated that muscular strength drops only four percent over a healthy person's lifetime. When you think that even Olympic aspirants tested at the Olympic Training Center were found to be out of condition, it seems conceivable that someone older could, with an intelligent and careful training program, reach a higher level of conditioning. I have found senior sailors very cunning, able to fall back on vast reservoirs of experience in strategy, tactics, and weather analysis. I think that these points have been borne out by the fact that senior sailors have won important national regattas and have done well in world competition.

How can you get more information about Masters sailing?

The national and international Laser class publications have most of the information regarding Masters regattas. Masters sailing is for everyone who is over 35 years of age. Come join us!

Recent Advances in Rigging Techniques

There have been a number of advances in rigging since my last discussion of sail controls found in chapter 3; what has fostered all this activity?

The introduction of the 3.8-ounce sail brought numerous rigging changes in the late 1980s. This material stretches less, so the new sail does not have as wide a range of shapes as the old 3.2-ounce sail. Most people agree that the new sail generates more power and necessitates depowering techniques earlier than the previous lighter sail. Most of the rigging changes have to do with the introduction of more purchase to the sail shape controls. This purchase has been added to the outhaul, cunningham, and boom vang.

Let's start with the outhaul.

The outhaul arrangement is shown in Figure A. Set up the clew as you have always done. After the line goes through the clam cleat, an eye-loop is tied into it in a position to act as a stopper for maximum release. The line is then led around the mast and another eye-loop is fashioned in the line. Two thimbles may be placed in the eye-loops to reduce friction on the line. The tail is threaded through the two eyes and left dangling down with a loop handle large enough for your hand so that you pull with your hand and wrist, not your fingers. This affords greater purchase and more convenience when controlling the outhaul.

How is the boom vang set up?

As shown in Figure A, the preferred vang arrangement is a simple 6:1 purchase. A swivel is necessary when attaching the jamming block onto the mast close to the deck. When tightening the vang upwind, trim the sail into the two-blocked position, cleat it, and use your foot to put pressure on the mainsheet between the ratchet block and the boom. As the boom bends down, use your forward hand to tighten the vang the required amount. The extra purchase also provides greater accuracy when easing the vang on reaches and runs, and in fact, the vang can be trimmed on the downwind legs. Spectron 12 line (or Dyneema in Europe), either ⅛-inch or ³⁄₁₆-inch, is ideal for the vang control. Here's how to rig the bilvang:

Step 1: On a table, place the larger jamming block on your left, with the swivel toward the left and the V jamming part toward you. Place the smaller becket block with the key 1 foot above and 2 feet to the right of the jamming block, key part to the right.

Step 2: Use 12 feet (14 feet if you want to make a rope handle) of ⅛- or ³⁄₁₆-inch (I prefer ⅛-inch) Spectron 12 line (called Dyneema in Europe). Measure 68 inches from one end of the line. Mark it with tape or marking pen.

Step 3: With the jamming block flat on the table, pass the end of the portion of the line through the top of the smaller hole of the jamming block and between the cheeks so that it exits toward you. Pull the line through so that the 68-inch mark is at the swivel. This controls the length of the vang and can later be adjusted as needed.

Step 4: Pass the end over the top of the swivel and around to the underneath side, then between the cheeks at the bottom and out the small hole on the underside of the block. This is a mirror image as in Step 3. Pull both lines tight and check to position your mark on top of the swivel.

Step 5: Pass the line through the becket of the key block (in a counterclockwise direction), then around the end sheave of the jamming block (counterclockwise direction), back to the key block and around its sheave (counterclockwise). Tie a 1-inch bowline loop at the end or use an optional block where rules permit. You are through with this part.

Step 6: Now, take the long end of the line, pass it through the bowline loop, or block if used, then back to the empty sheave (counterclockwise) of the jamming block and exit through the V of the jam. Make a 6-inch handle at the end with a bowline, or, by using another 2 feet of line, tie a series of truckers knots, pulling the line through the last truckers knot to finish off with a bowline back on itself to complete the rope handle.

How do you handle the cunningham?

Another aid to trimming the firmer sail is putting more purchase on the cunningham. A tight cunningham helps keep the draft forward and the leech open, helping heavy-air handling. Figure A demonstrates an 8:1 purchase, all with one line as required by the class rules. Three plastic or steel thimbles are allowed to reduce friction and wear on the line. However, use of

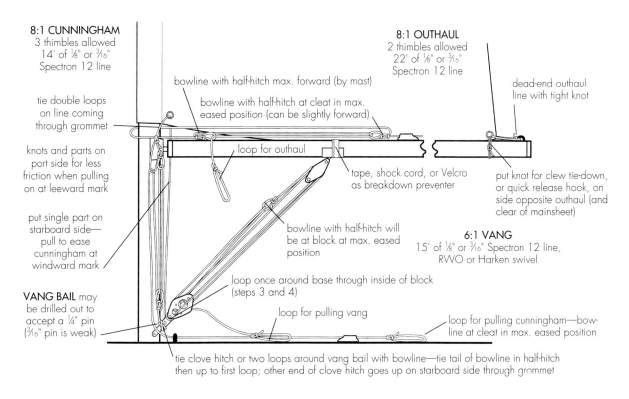

8:1 CUNNINGHAM
3 thimbles allowed
14' of ⅛" or ³⁄₁₆"
Spectron 12 line

tie double loops
on line coming
through grommet

knots and parts on
port side for less
friction when pulling
on at leeward mark

put single part on
starboard side—
pull to ease
cunningham at
windward mark

VANG BAIL may
be drilled out to
accept a ¼" pin
(³⁄₁₆" pin is weak)

bowline with half-hitch max. forward (by mast)

bowline with half-hitch at cleat in max.
eased position (can be slightly forward)

loop for outhaul

tape, shock cord, or Velcro
as breakdown preventer

bowline with half-hitch will
be at block at max. eased
position

loop once around base through inside of block
(steps 3 and 4)

loop for pulling vang

tie clove hitch or two loops around vang bail with bowline—tie tail of bowline in half-hitch
then up to first loop; other end of clove hitch goes up on starboard side through grommet

8:1 OUTHAUL
2 thimbles allowed
22' of ⅛" or ³⁄₁₆"
Spectron 12 line

dead-end outhaul
line with tight knot

put knot for clew tie-down,
or quick release hook, on
side opposite outhaul (and
clear of mainsheet)

6:1 VANG
15' of ⅛" or ³⁄₁₆" Spectron 12 line,
RWO or Harken swivel

loop for pulling cunningham—bowline at cleat in max. eased position

Figure A. Laser rigging adjustments.

Spectron 12 line can eliminate the need for thimbles. The cunningham starts coming on early when you first start hiking. As the wind and waves build, the cunningham should be getting tighter until the grommet is at or below the gooseneck in extreme conditions.

The hiking strap can now be adjusted; how do you set yours up?

Figure B shows this arrangement. One-quarter-inch Marlow prestretch line is dead-ended at the starboard eyestrap and is drawn through the loop in the end of the hiking strap. An eye-loop is tied into the line at a point where, if this loop were adjacent to the end of the hiking strap, the strap would be set for the helmsman's fully hiked position. The tail is threaded through the port eyestrap, then through the eye-loop, and finally through the starboard eyestrap. A hand loop is made in the line using a bowline. This setup makes the hiking strap infinitely adjustable. The controlling hand loop is set on the starboard side of the boat so that the helmsperson can, after rounding the windward mark, reach down to pull the line and the hiking strap taut. This gives better hiking leverage and control for the reaches. Before the leeward mark, he or she may have to lean in for a second and pull the line between the eyestraps to loosen it to the upwind setting. By the way, the precautions discussed on page 33 regarding the hiking strap still hold true.

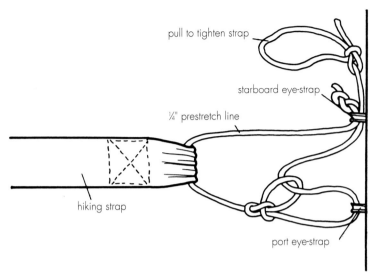

pull to tighten strap

starboard eye-strap

¼" prestretch line

hiking strap

port eye-strap

Figure B. Hiking strap adjustment.

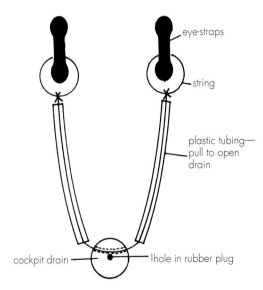

eye-straps

string

plastic tubing—
pull to open
drain

cockpit drain

hole in rubber plug

Figure C. Bird's-eye view of a cockpit bailer adjustment device.

Do you have a tip on storing gear?

As you might imagine, storing gear on your Laser can be a problem. Probably the easiest solution to this dilemma is to insert two 6-inch in-spection ports on each side of the centerboard trunk. One, on the starboard side, is usually sufficient. A shock cord can be stretched and secured close to the deck around the centerboard trunk in the interior of the boat. A water bottle, sponge, bag of spare parts or food, or spray top, can be draped over the shock cord and kept relatively dry. Storage bags can be inserted in the inspection ports for further storage if needed.

Referring to the bailer discussed on page 37, has anyone suggested a better way to open it?

Opening a closed cockpit bailer in heavy weather can be a real trick, particularly for the senior sailor. A device has been rigged up to help in this situation. Figure C shows a string or a light cable leading from the eyestrap at the back of the cockpit, down through the rubber plug of the cockpit drain, and back to the other eye-strap. In those segments between the plug and the eyestraps, the line has been drawn through some small plastic tubing. To open the drain, a person must only reach the eyestrap at the back of the cockpit, pull forward on the plastic tubing, and the rubber plug will be pulled forward to open the drain.

Tips on Maintenance

Leaks are the cause for most maintenance problems; how do you find them?

To find a leak, place a small piece of tape over the vent hole underneath the hiking strap in the forward wall of the cockpit. Very soapy water should be placed on all fittings, into the centerboard trunk, and around the cockpit drain. Blow air into the hull through the stern drain hole; use the exhaust of a vacuum cleaner, but be careful not to introduce too much air into the hull, since this could cause separation of certain glued surfaces in the interior of the boat. Then carefully examine all areas of the boat for soap bubbles. This procedure helps find any areas where water might infiltrate the interior of the hull. Carefully caulk these areas with sealant, allow the sealant to dry, and repeat the process again until the hull is airtight. Remember to remove the tape from the vent hole when you finish.

What if you've looked for leaks as described above and find none, but your boat still leaks when you sail?

Then you must suspect the mast step as the source of the leak. Cracks in the mast step usually do not open up until stress is put on the structure by the mast while sailing. Put a heavy-duty plastic bag into the mast step and adhere the edge of the top of the bag to the hull using duct tape. Place the mast carefully into the mast step, then sail upwind with the mainsheet two-blocked in fairly heavy conditions. Try not to tack and jibe too much, since the bag may rip. If the hull is dry when you return to shore, then your leak is in the mast step.

What makes the mast step start to leak?

The mast step can be damaged in a number of ways. A violent death roll in heavy air can put enormous force on the base of the step. Allowing the bottom of the mast to pound into the base of the step when the boat is tipped over in shallow water is another good cause for cracking. Sand and grit, if allowed to accumulate in the base of the step, can wear through the gelcoat and fiberglass layers as the mast rotates.

How is the mast step of a Laser constructed?

The mast step is designed in a peculiar way (Figure D). It is constructed as an extrusion from the deck. This closed-in fiberglass tube is pushed down into a glob of water-resistant, Bondo-type material in a plywood doughnut that is glassed into the interior of the hull. When the mast step becomes permeable, water infiltrates the Bondo material, degrading it. Finally, the Bondo material loosens from the plywood doughnut. If the Bondo material becomes quite loose, the mast step will break out of the plywood doughnut, and the deck and step will break as the mast falls down.

How can you repair the mast step?

You can buy the repair kit described on page 87 at your Laser dealer, or you can fix it yourself. To repair it yourself, cut a 6-inch inspection port into the deck approximately 30 centimeters away from the entrance for the mast. Remove the Bondo material from around the base. When it does not come out easily, a chisel can sometimes be used. A high-speed hobby drill is useful to remove the Bondo material within the plywood doughnut. The dust which this produces should be removed immediately with a vacuum cleaner and the area cleaned with acetone. A small amount of acetone should be poured into the mast step entrance on the deck. These areas should be dried; a heat gun may be useful. Fiberglass strips impregnated with a minimum amount of epoxy or polyester should be wrapped around the base of the mast step and compressed into the space between the step and the plywood doughnut. Before this mixture goes off, the mast rake and position should be checked to make sure that they have not changed during the repair process. A small amount of epoxy should be carefully poured into the bottom of the mast step so that 2–3 millimeters covers the bottom and seals off any cracks. Without further abuse the boat should be dry and good as new.

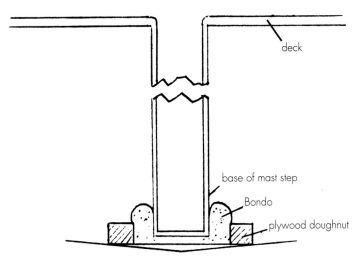

Figure D. Laser mast step construction.

Any other places where serious leaks may occur and can be repaired?

The second most common source for serious leaks in the Laser is the cockpit drain. This is usually caused by improper trailering. The earlier boats had a plastic fitting through this hole, whereas the newer boats have a threaded brass fitting. The cockpit drain hole is drilled through the fiberglass layer of the cockpit wall and also the fiberglass hull skin, making it a convenient route for water leaking into the boat. In order to repair this leak, the fitting must be removed from the drain. The space between the two fiberglass layers, which has been filled with a Bondo-like material, should be cleaned out. This is most easily done by a high-speed hobby tool fitted with a small, thin grinding wheel. The wheel must have a smaller diameter than the drain hole. This wheel is used to ream out the layer of degenerated Bondo in the space between the two fiberglass walls. The area is washed with acetone and dried. Water-resistant epoxy putty is introduced into the space and packed as well as possible on all sides. Epoxy putty is placed on the brass fitting, and this is inserted back into the cockpit drain hole. Make sure that all spaces are filled with the putty. The brass nut is then tightened onto the fitting. Excess putty is wiped away and the area is allowed to cure. If done properly, this procedure should afford years of vigorous use without further leakage from this area.

Minor repairs of the centerboard and rudder are discussed on page 89. If these foils warp, how are they straightened?

The stock centerboard that comes with the Laser is almost perfect. Some sanding may be needed when there are imperfections in the production process. Foils may warp when exposed to extreme high temperatures, as in the trunk of a car. After some time, many boards need to be straightened. The foil is placed in a padded bench vise with the trailing edge pointing upward. Find two straight hardwood 1 × 6 boards approximately the length of the foil. With a propane torch, carefully heat the warped area. The torch must be moved continuously, otherwise it will burn the foam gel material of which the board is made. The area will eventually turn from a solid to a rubbery consistency. Place the wood boards on both sides of the trailing edge of the foil and clamp firmly. Allow the foil to cool. It may be necessary to repeat this procedure several times. When the board is straight, remove the planks, sand the areas, and cover with either gelcoat or West System epoxy. Sand the area again until smooth.

Zigzagging Downwind

ED ADAMS

Ed Adams has been a part of the Laser racing scene since its inception. He logged a number of victories in the early years of the class including wins at the U.S. Nationals and British Nationals. A two-time Rolex Yachtsman of the Year, Adams also has won the Star Worlds, J/24 and Snipe North Americans, and the Collegiate North Americans. More recently, as the 1996 US SAILING Coach, he worked with Nick Adamson, who won the U.S. Olympic Trials and sailed the Laser as it made its debut in the Savannah Olympics. In this capacity, Ed observed and descibes here the remarkable downwind techniques perfected by Adamson, which the top sailors are now using.

Assuming a Laser sailor has mastered the basic boat handling skills for sailing downwind, what additional skills are needed to get to the bottom mark even faster?

The first skill you need to master is sailing by the lee. But realize that mainsheet trim by the lee varies with the wind strength. In light air, it pays to ease the boom well past perpendicular. As the wind builds, the sheet should be eased less and less, and trimmed well aft of perpendicular in heavy air (over 15 knots). Over-easing the sheet in more wind will often cause a capsize.

The second skill to master is knowing when to make wave riding the priority. In light air, or when the wind is offshore, waves travel slowly. You should ignore them and sail straight at the mark.

As the windspeed or fetch increases, so does the speed of the waves. In most moderate, onshore breeze conditions, the waves will be traveling faster than your flat water boatspeed. Then it will pay to zigzag—hunting, catching, and riding waves. Don't hunt unless you see something worth catching.

Once the wind builds to the point where you are planing all the time, your speed can exceed that of the waves. Then your goal is to sail toward the mark as directly as possible, avoiding the steep waves.

When hunting for waves to ride in moderate air, speed makes the job easier. By reaching up as a wave approaches, you build the speed required to jump onto the wave face. When the wave lifts your transom, bear off to grab the ride. Don't sail directly down the wave. If you can sail across the wave face like a surfer, you can attain higher speeds while still making the same progress dead downwind, toward the mark. That extra speed comes in handy when it's time to turn off that wave and hunt for your next ride.

In a boat with an unstayed rig, you can sail across the wave face two ways: on a reach or by the lee, as there are no shrouds to restrict how far you can ease the mainsheet. This two-directional ability gives you twice as much territory in which to hunt waves. The turn down to by the lee is called a *top turn*, because it is done at the top of a wave, as it lifts your transom. The turn up is called a *bottom turn*, because it is usually done just before you reach the trough of the wave you are riding.

How do tactical considerations and wind strength come into play for the downwind leg?

First, consider the wind strength. If it is out-of-control windy, approach the run as you would in a keelboat: get on the long jibe that takes you on a broad reach toward the leeward mark. Reaching provides you a wider choice of angles to avoid slow-moving waves. Sailing by the lee is too angle-critical; you're likely to plow into a wave and capsize.

However, in any other wind strength, do the opposite of what the sailing books say: get on the lifted jibe. If you come into the weather mark in a left-hand shift, jibe onto port so you can be by the lee immediately, while pointing most directly at the mark. If you're not sure which shift you're on, don't worry about it—you'll go just about as fast whether you reach or sail by the lee. Pressure and waves are far more important.

Clear air does matter, as better pressure always means better speed. But lateral freedom is just as important. In wave-riding conditions, you need to have at least 100 feet of space on either side of you, so your bottom and top turns can be made without restriction from other boats. So pick a course that gets you away from the crowd early.

Finally, get out on the water and put in your practice time. Wave riding is a high-wire act. Like skiing, the only way to negotiate a mogul field is with perfect, fearless balance and with confidence born of many hours and countless capsizes.

A top turn is done at the top of a wave, as it lifts your transom. How would you describe negotiating a top turn?

Prior to a top turn, look for a wave approaching from your weather quarter. Reach up to build the speed necessary to jump onto the wave. A second before the wave arrives, initiate the top turn. The first step is to ease the mainsheet and let the boat roll to weather. This windward roll is accentuated as the wave begins to lift the transom. The roll allows the boat to bear off naturally, without any help from the rudder. Don't fight the turn!

The action of catching a wave is a controlled near-capsize to weather. As the boat rolls to weather, resist the instinct to fight the roll with a jab of the tiller to leeward; a jab adds drag to the turn and the wave is often lost. Some sailors try to pump the mainsheet as they turn down, or use the tiller to bear off sharply, which accentuates the pump. This rarely works, and usually throws the sailor off balance, requiring

further jabs of the tiller to regain control. A good top turn is a smooth roll with no tiller pressure. Expect to capsize while learning to perfect this part of the turn.

To finish the top turn, the trick is to come out of it on the correct course so the boat levels out naturally, without any tiller jabs to leeward. The correct course lets the boat ride across the wave face without *bottoming out* (reaching the trough) prematurely. The mainsheet should be eased just enough so the telltales show reverse (leech to luff) flow; any further ease will result in an "over-trimmed sail" (because the flow is reversed.) Common mistakes are raising the board too high and over-easing the sheet, both of which make the boat unstable. If the boat gets "wobbly", it requires tiller correction, which adds drag and forces the boat off the correct wave-riding course.

Now let's examine a bottom turn, which is done just before you reach the trough of the wave. How do you handle that?

Prior to a bottom turn, you are sailing by the lee, riding a wave. Looking ahead, you see that your wave is getting chopped up—losing its form. Before the wave dies, begin a bottom turn. Sometimes your turn up can put you back on the wave you were just riding. Or you can turn toward the mark if no waves are worth chasing. Other times you can continue reaching after the turn if you see another good wave approaching. A common mistake is to milk the original wave too long; the wave either dies or the boat rides into its trough, planting the bow into the next wave. Either way, it becomes harder to turn up onto a reach. Every bottom turn must be initiated by putting the helm to leeward; to overcome the drag of the rudder it must be done early, while the boat is still moving fast and the bow is lifted clear of the water.

As you progress through the bottom turn, air flow reattaches to the sail, with the telltales streaming from luff to leech. As the helm is put down, the boat naturally rolls to leeward. Let it roll; this will help the boat turn. In the initial part of the bottom turn, center your body on the edge of the cockpit to let the boat heel. The earlier the bottom turn began on the previous wave, the faster the boat can spin toward the wind. You should be able to spin the boat so fast that you have to lean out against the centrifugal force. Being forced to lean inboard throughout the spin is a sign that the turn was begun too late.

As you complete the bottom turn, trim the mainsheet as hard and as fast as possible. Because you are turning through 60 degrees or more, this means trimming from knee to shoulder, using alternate hands, four to six times. Hand speed is the key here. Practice and time in the boat will help to develop these techniques.

World Class Downwind and Upwind Techniques

LUTHER CARPENTER

Luther Carpenter has been a coach for the U.S. Sailing Team since 1989. He has worked extensively with the Europe Dinghy class, the Laser class, the 49er class, and the 470. Carpenter's background in Olympic class dinghies started with two 470 campaigns in 1984 and 1988. In 1988, he and teammate Joe Bersch were selected as tuning partners for the eventual Bronze medalists at the Seoul Olympics, John Shadden and Charlie Mckee. It was during this intensive training period that Carpenter became addicted to boatspeed, tuning, and analyzing technique and sail shape. Since 1989, Carpenter has succesfully coached at two Olympics, with Julia Trotman (1992) and Courtenay Becker (1996) both winning Bronze medals in the Europe Class.

When coaching the Laser class, Carpenter enjoys observing the best sailors at events and then goes home to experiment with his observations in his own Laser. "While the Laser is a very non-technical class, I enjoy really figuring out the intricacies of the boat, and know-

ing why we are seeing the different speeds and techniques used on the race course. Winning races is always easier if you have a boatspeed advantage!

We learned in chapter 6, Advanced Techniques Offwind, of the speed advantages in playing the waves. You have put a name to this: S-Curving. Give us a description of this concept and technique.

Without a doubt, the biggest change to Laser sailing in the last seven years is the importance and emphasis on downwind performance. The goal of Olympic performance in Savannah, and the emphasis on running in the trapezoid courses, demanded a new attitude toward non-stop surfing and planing. The highest achievers developed a technique called S-Curving, which is a combination of sailing broad reach and by the lee angles. While we find it easy to casually let the term *S-Curving* roll off our tongues, it is the most complex technique to describe, practice, and execute, in sailboat racing today.

The concept is fairly basic. Broad reaching and by the lee angles provide more load and flow over the sail than straight running. Frequently, this is the extra required power that is needed to initiate a surf down a wave. The added bonus is that these two angles provide more stability, so we can sail the boat aggressively, knowing that the side forces are always defined—there is no question which way the boat wants to heel or capsize.

On a square running leg, the challenge is to combine the two modes to continuously surf down the leg, while smoothly changing from broad reaching to by the lee. This transition is the first skill to aquire when developing good S-Curving technique. It is tricky because the force on the rig reverses, requiring a weight change while negotiating perfect steering and sheeting of the sail. A fast Laser sailor can make this transition flow smoothly, and utilize the exchange in heel and pressure in a powerful kinetic movement, much like exiting a roll tack.

When sailors are developing S-Curving skills, I usually ask them to focus on wide angles and a fast exchange from one mode to the other. I speak of developing a rhythm for the turns, which emphasizes the body's reaction to the rate of turn. It is essential that the mainsheet movements *lead* the turn, for the sail trim defines the rate of turn and develops the pressure to move your weight against. As you steer into each new mode, you are hoping to achieve maximum load on the sheet, and this can only be achieved by perfect mainsheet trimming and easing.

Most sailors find the broad reaching angle easy to find, while the by the lee is a bit more elusive. We run into trouble because we don't realize that continuing to bear off and easing the sheet builds pressure when going into the by the lee mode. Many sailors feel the tension on the sheet dying as they bear off, and mistakenly stop the turn too early and end up with no tension on the sheet. Keep the turns fast and wide at first for positive tension and load.

The transferring of weight during the S-Curving maneuver is another difficult skill to master. Most Laser sailors have one of two stances downwind: aft knee up, or aft knee down. Both modes work, but each caters slightly better toward one of the two angles. Aft knee up is the natural position most of us use while reaching. It feels very normal and facilitates easy hiking against the strap or leeward handrail, if needed. The downside of this mode is that it is extremely difficult to get weight to leeward when the boat heels up to windward. You must push hard on your feet on the leeward side of the cockpit floor to keep the boat from capsizing to windward. This mode tends to feel more out of control when by the lee, which can sometimes force you to sail angles closer to running. Be-

cause the body is extra sensitive to windward heel and wind angle, this position can be deadly fast when running in light air, because we tend to wander too far into the by the lee zone.

The aft-knee-down mode is best for traveling extreme angles and long distances by the lee. The knee down allows for the chest to easily travel across the boat and enable extreme weight to leeward. Knee-down connoisseurs like to use their hands to push down on the leeward rail for explosive acceleration when needed. The downside of the knee-down position is that it limits the "high" point of your cycle—when heading up to broad reaching, it's not as easy to switch smoothly to hiking the boat flat with power.

You mentioned the rhythm of S-Curving. Can you explain in more detail why you use this term?

Although we talk about the two modes and the rhythm from one to the other, it's essential to understand that S-Curving is not a repetitive transition back and forth on every wave. As we progress down the run we experience different waves running at different angles, as well as the wind shifting. These two changing factors require lots of quick thinking and reactions to ride the waves. One might find a set of three waves that can be surfed by the lee, and then have the wind head slightly, opening the door to surfing while broad reaching for a few waves. The ability to change your mind and react to each wave and puff is essential to good downwind performance. One mode is always better than the other, and we must choose the correct one on the fly.

In the real world, this translates into usually a three-wave ride in one direction, and then a one- or two-wave ride in the other. I find it helpful to think about the ratio on each different day; yesterday was 4:2, today might be 1:5 (broad reaching straight down the waves, only occasionally sailing by the lee.) It's important to research and realize each day's wind and wave relationship before the race, and select the best possible mode for surfing: starboard broad reaching; starboard by the lee; port broad reaching; port by the lee.

What is an example of this?

Here is a personal example of a typical race I sailed. During my pre-race routine, I found it easiest to catch waves on starboard tack by the lee. The wind was in a dying trend, so I knew catching waves early on the run was going to be important. On the run I had the lead and worked about five waves in a row by the lee, finding marginal surfing on most waves. As I surfed low of the fleet, I waited for either a lull, when surfing would no longer be possible, or a header, to make my move back in front of the fleet to realize my gain. Lulls were more common, so I would reach fairly aggressively back in front of the fleet with good speed. Since my speed was decent in the lulls, as soon as the puffs returned I could immediately drop down by the lee again and catch another wave, and so on. In this way I made sure I was combining both modes at the appropriate time, and stayed in touch with the fleet while extending my lead.

Twice in this example I was incredibly "in sync" with the waves and puffs and went quite well on the runs. Other times I was searching for the pattern—some of us can be so harsh as to call that *flailing*, i.e., I was going up when I should have been going down. When you buy in to the S-Curving formula, you must realize that sometimes you will have things backwards for a few waves, or sometimes the wave-catching ability is just not there, and it may be faster to put the bow on the mark. But if S-Curve conditions *do* exist, the ones who can dominate! I guarantee you will love it as you develop it. The most important tip I can give is to teach yourself in the most radical way possible—the wider the angles you sail, the faster you will learn.

Your explanation is convincing enough, but can you describe a way to develop S-Curving skills while at the same time avoiding costly capsizes?

You know the basic ingredients for avoiding the death roll—sheet in and head up. The important point is to examine the actual angle that you are sailing. Lasers are most prone to instability when sailed from broad reaching to dead down-wind. This zone is incredibly unstable due to the nature of the forces on the rig—will the boat heel to windward or leeward? The awkwardness of this feeling contributes to a cautious skipper, hoping for more survival than speed.

This zone has also been proven to be the slowest point of sail in the Laser. So it is a lethal combination—slow and unstable. The creation of the S-Curve technique is really the result of the avoidance of this zone. When S-Curving we are traveling from by the lee, an extremely stable and usually good wave riding angle, to a rapid transition up to broad reaching. The more we linger in the death zone, the slower and more vulnerable we are.

Speed is the most important component of stability. While over-trimming can also prevent capsizes, the real answer is to challenge yourself with the S-Curve technique. Start by beam reaching (or slightly lower), and then rapidly but smoothly bear down to by the lee. It is imperative that you ease the sheet at the same rate you turn, and also move your body inboard. A little hawk, or similar wind indicator, is very valuable for developing this skill. Practice this skill first in 10 knots and flat water and really go for it. See how extreme you can get with the angles. Then slowly add more breeze and waves to the formula. When going from by the lee to broad reaching transition, the most important skill to develop is sheeting in enough mainsheet. If you head up faster than you trim, you will be swimming.

S-Curving is the technique that transfers Laser sailors from being fearful to going like rocket ships off the wind. Learn to love it, find the rhythm, and practice it in an extreme fashion. After all, when you've just finished a grinding gut-wrenching beat, the last thing you need is an anxiety trip down to the leeward mark! Plane and surf by them instead, feeling loose and fast.

Now that we understand S-Curving, what can you tell us about the kinetics the top sailors are using to enhance their technique?

The Laser's basic sail plan begs for kinetic movement. The tall and whippy mast bends and returns quickly while going upwind, and the actual weight and springy motion downwind keeps the leech bouncing or pumping.

When S-Curving, the angle of heel is changing a lot and often, which is when the top sailors are taking advantage of the transitions. They let the boat steer through the large angles with heel and then force the boat flat, which gives them the added burst of speed necessary to catch the waves that are marginal for a surf. When the top guys get completely in sync, these motions get amplified by the spar's natural tendency to spring back and forth. It's a beautiful thing to watch, and extremely satisfying to achieve when in your own boat.

Large pumps on the mainsheet are very efficient when moving into broad reaching mode, while very short eases and mini-trims will generate extra power when by the lee. And if you are in the knee-down mode, don't forget about pushing down that leeward rail with your hands if the boat needs a swift flattening. That's acceleration!

Now let's talk about going upwind. Chapter 5, Advanced Techniques Upwind, discussed the benefits of torquing and proper weight positioning for going fast. As the US SAILING coach, you have observed and helped our top sailors go upwind in waves. How much steering should be done with the body, and how much with the tiller?

I have found it very helpful to experiment with the raw effects of weight movement regardless of waves. Putting weight forward pushes the bow down in the water, thus increasing the waterline. This tends to create more weather helm and power, both great for pointing. The boat should feel like the groove is tight and narrow with the bow pressed down in this manner. Most of us load our forward legs in the hiking strap and lean our forward shoulder down and forward to achieve this mode. The downside of this mode is that the boat can slow down quickly if we make a steering or hiking error.

Shifting weight aft shortens the waterline by raising the v-bow out of the water. This gives us a loose or wide groove, which is great for producing the fast forward mode. The boat feels lively and accelerates forward versus rounding up. The most common stance to achieve weight aft is to load the aft thigh, and roll the shoulders *out* and back.

The next time you go sailing in puffy, full power, flat-water conditions, experiment with these two different modes. You should find that the aft shoulder mode will enable you to sail through the puffs with less mainsheet ease than when you are leaning forward. The slowest mode in breeze upwind is mediocre hiking forward in the cockpit, leaning forward to rest while easing the mainsheet. This is exactly what all of us do when we get tired. Knowing and reminding yourself of these facts help force you to rotate your hiking from leg to leg, increasing the blood flow in your legs and providing a better balance between the speed and height modes.

What is an example of this?

Let's pretend we are sailing upwind in a 12- to 18-knot offshore wind. The chop is relatively short, but the puffs and lulls are severe and quick. We read an approaching puff and pull on the anticipated vang tension required, one to two boat lengths before the puff strikes. As the puff hits, we discover it is a lift and quickly respond with a sharp hard hike on our aft thigh as we steer up. We ease the mainsheet only during the first boat length of the puff and then come block to block as our new course in the lift settles down. As soon as things are stable and the helm is neutral, we roll into equal tension on both legs and continue to hike through the puff. As the puff dies, we ease the vang while leaning forward, loading the forward leg. Depending on the chop, we continue either slightly heeled or flat. The slightly heeled and weight forward mode is extremely effective for pointing and power in the lulls and chop. The bonus of this position is that it keeps your butt out over the water, and the load on your front thigh gives the aft power thigh a break in anticipation of the next puff. As the next puff approaches, get ready . . . 3–2–1 - wham!, aft thigh loaded, shoulders held *straight out* and aft. Truck through the puff, feel the burn of your stomach and legs, and enjoy the spray as you blast upwind nice and flat.

Once you understand and feel this technique in an offshore wind condition, you can slowly develop good technique in larger waves. Impact with the waves requires an aft speed mode, while using the flat spaces in between the waves for pointing—forward weight mode. As you crest over a wave, load the aft thigh quickly, helping to push the bow deeper into the wave and keeping the bow from crashing back down into the water—it shouldn't catch air. We all know that keeping the bow traveling through a smooth track of water is fast—pounding bows is hateful and tends to scoop water into the cockpit. The hardest part of developing good technique is that most of us lack the power that needs to be delivered to the aft thigh over and over. This is where the speed comes from when overpowered, so set your goals to increase the frequency and force you spend fully extended in the aft mode.

Now let's talk about tiller movement in light air and chop.

Usually in conditions below max power—full hiking—we are trying to keep rudder movement to a minimum to avoid drag. In light air with chop, there will obviously be some helm movement required. I like to think about the actual size of the waves. Are they just bumpy chop that slow the boat down, or are they left over from recent higher winds, creating larger waves than the breeze conditions? The latter condition tends to deliver waves that peak over the lip of the bow and can possibly send water back to the cockpit. As we all know, this is something to be avoided. The rule is, anything goes to keep the bow out of the water. Aggressive steering here is OK, sometimes even if it is out of sync with our body movements. We also try to see not only the wave we are cresting, but the next two waves as well. If we view the waves in these sets, we can do more steering around the bigger waves, even at the expense of losing some

height (pointing). As I developed as a helmsman growing up, I constantly heard the great sailors talk about this "steering around" concept, but it took me several years to actually abandon my perfect telltale groove quest for the smoother path through the water. Of course, when I did start looking at the sets instead of just *my* wave, my wave technique became a real weapon of speed. Tiller movements should relate directly to body movements and heel: heeling to leeward to head up, flattening for neutral helm or bearing off. Keeping the leeward telltale from stalling is key to maintaining speed.

What would a typical cycle of rudder movement look like?

Approaching a wave, bear off just slightly, with a small heel to leeward and a slight ease on sheet. As the wave passes underneath the mast step, do a shoulder extension coupled with a fast trim on the sheet—power on with the sheet, speeding forward through the wave with mast deflection and snap of the rig. Now glance at the leeward telltale to see where you are. If the telltale is shaky or drooping, ease the sheet and heel to leeward while beginning to head up. As boat speeds up, trim and pressure down with butt and shoulder extension. Then anticipate the next wave. As long as you are in sync, even though there are helm movements, the helm should flow and feel little resistance. Even though our body motions may be quick and assertive, we want to avoid jabbing and pulling the tiller with force.

What about kinetic movement upwind? What are you seeing the top sailors doing?

Upwind the problem is that the Laser's traveler does not enable the boom to go far enough to leeward. This makes the boat very difficult to sail. The boat always wants to point and stall instead of going fast forward. The upper mast's ability to sidebend quickly helps to keep the boat moving forward fast and is the main reason for kinetic movement upwind. The harder you sheet the mainsheet, the more important this factor becomes. We see this technique used most often in light air and choppy conditions, where sailors sheet hard to point but throw their weight against that sheeting for rig deflection and acceleration forward. It is the basic movement that every Laser should and usually does have. When the mainsheet comes in, you automatically hike against it. The faster the sheet comes in, the more assertive the hike must be.

The top-level sailors take this concept one step further by incorporating the previously mentioned fore versus aft weight ideas and adding the kinetic movement. We see Robert Scheidt and Ben Ainslie often combining the magical three components: forward speed, height, and power created by cresting waves with an assertive hike on the aft thigh (for speed) while steering up—pointing—to find the easiest and smoothest track over the wave. Their tiller motions up can be quite quick in this sequence, and surely feel wrong when first attempting the technique. However, practice and careful matching of powerful hiking to steering will begin to deliver the desired effect.

Kinetics is a strange word in the Laser class. Everyone throws the term around, yet few describe what they actually do. The borderline nature of kinetics is surely the culprit of this *speak-no-evil* attitude. Most of us know the difference between laziness and cheating. I know that more often than not, I'm being lazy in the cockpit of my boat and am tempted to accuse those being more physical than I of cheating. My belief is that an open dialogue about kinetics will permit us all to sail on a more level playing field, and ultimately the sailors and the level of judging will determine the gray areas.

And a final question. For the world-class sailor, say perhaps the top one-half percent, is mast and sail selection a big thing?

A basic understanding of the Laser rig needs to be thought about when pursuing top-notch gear. The top section is too bendy, and the bottom section is too stiff for an even bend and consistent control of the sail shape. So as Laser sailors there are a few things we must focus on to try and obtain top performance from our equipment.

Since the top section is the major culprit of the problem, make sure that your top section is in good shape. A straight section with excellent tight collars is essential. Go to extreme lengths to get that mast joint as snug as possible. Packing tape on a loose fitting collar works, or better yet, replace the loose collar with a tight new one. I have found the collars from the Australian masts to be excellent.

The age of the mast does not necessarily relate to stiffness. Most actually believe that a new spar is potentially bendy and can become permanently bent if used in a big blow early in its life. Metal experts claim that the material hardens after being slowly flexed. So most of us are careful to use new spars in a break-in period, and avoid extreme vang or stuffing of the bow into waves with a new spar.

The most common problem I see is sailors using a spar that is just gone. It has been bent and just doesn't provide a stiff enough tension to sheet the sail against. These sailors usually have to ease their outhaul excessively to make up for the lost power and are constantly battling the clew-to-mast-joint wrinkle. From the coach boat, it's easy to see who has a good rig. The better rigs can be seen with a tighter outhaul, yet still have great power and pointing.

The last item to mention is obviously the sail. Because of the power lost due to the bendy top section, most Laser sailors are looking for a sail that provides a tight firm leech and has minimal leech flutter. The recent trend has been to favor the British sails, said to be made from stiffer cloth. The U.S. manufacturer has followed this trend and is currently changing its sails to use the same guidelines as the British.

Whichever sail you use, I coach the obvious—for the big events, use a fresh sail. Laser sails are incredibly inexpensive compared to other one-design classes, and the difference of using a new sail is noticeable. I see a big difference in light air, so if you are on a budget, use your brand new sail in light air regattas, and your next best sail in breezier conditions.

Laser Championship Record

Following are selected 1990–1999 results. Thanks to the International Laser Class Association for the use of the archive results pages on their website, <*http://www. laserinternational.org/archives.htm*>.

OLYMPIC GAMES

1996 SAVANNAH, USA
1st Robert Scheidt BRA
2nd Ben Ainslie GBR
3rd Peer Moberg NOR
4th Michael Blackburn AUS
5th Stefan Warkalla GER

WORLD CHAMPIONSHIPS
Excepting 1980, entry to the Senior World Championships (Standard Rig) is restricted.

1999 MELBOURNE, AUSTRALIA
1st Ben Ainslie GBR
2nd Robert Scheidt BRA
3rd Karl Suneson SWE
4th Michael Blackburn AUS
5th Andrew Simpson GBR

1998 MEDEMBLIK, NETHERLANDS

Laser Radial—Male
1st Gustavo Lima POR
2nd Andonis Bougiouris GRE
3rd Alexandros Logothetis GRE
4th Raimondas Siugzdinis LTU
5th Luca Radelic CRO

Laser Radial—Youth
1st Alastair Gair NZL
2nd Evagelos Himonas GRE
3rd Goncalo Gonzalez Lopes POR
4th Leigh McMillan GBR
5th David Hiver GBR

Laser Radial—Women
1st Larissa Nevierov ITA
2nd Carolijn Brouwer NED
3rd Jeanette Dagson SWE
4th Marcelien de Koning NED
5th Jo Dikkenberg AUS

1997 ALGARROBO, CHILE
1st Robert Scheidt BRA
2nd Nik Burfoot NZL
3rd Ben Ainslie GBR
4th Hamish Pepper NZL
5th Hugh Styles GBR

1997 MOHEMEDIA, MOROCCO

Laser Radial—Male
1st Raimondas Siugzdinis LTU
2nd Romain Knipping FRA
3rd Selim Kakis TUR
4th Benoit Raphalen FRA
5th Goncalo Lopes POR

Laser Radial—Youth
1st Teddy Questroy FRA
2nd Romain Knipping FRA
3rd Alaistair Gair NZL
4th Justin Deal GBR
5th Joac Santos Silva POR

Laser Radial—Women
1st Sarah Blanck AUS
2nd Helen Waite GBR
3rd Anja Sahlberg SWE
4th Anje de Boer NED
5th Larissa Nevierov ITA

1996 SIMON'S TOWN, SOUTH AFRICA
1st Robert Scheidt BRA
2nd Karl Suneson SWE
3rd Ben Ainslie GBR
4th Stefan Warkalla GER
5th Iain Percy GBR

Laser Radial
1st Brendan Casey AUS
2nd Andrew Kiriljuk RUS
3rd Allan Coutts NZL
4th Tim Shuwalow AUS
5th Dimitris Theodorakis GRE

Women
1st Jacqueline Ellis AUS
2nd Larissa Nevierov ITA
3rd Kathryn McQueen AUS
4th Sarah Blanck AUS
5th Alison Casey AUS

1995 TENERIFE, CANARY ISLANDS
1st Robert Scheidt BRA
2nd Nik Burfoot NZL
3rd Eivind Melleby NOR
4th Hamish Pepper NZL
5th Michael Blackburn AUS

Laser Radial
1st Brendan Casey AUS
2nd Tim Shuwalow AUS
3rd Gustavo Roxo de Lima POR
4th Sean Kirkjian AUS
5th David Huet FRA

Women
1st Heidi Gordon AUS
2nd Larissa Nevierov ITA
3rd Roberta Hartley GBR

4th Alison Casey AUS
5th Roelien Huisman NED

1994 WAKAYAMA, JAPAN
1st Nikolas Burfoot NZL
2nd Pascal Lacoste FRA
3rd Serge Kats NED
4th Hamish Pepper NZL
5th Peer Moberg NOR

Women
1st Melanie Dennison AUS
2nd Jacqueline Ellis AUS
3rd Tracey Tan SIN
4th Ma. Bettina Marcone ARG
5th Elizabeth Roberts AUS

Laser Radial
1st Rui Pedro Coelho POR
2nd Rodion Luka UKR
3rd Nahtan Handley NZL
4th Yanghe Zhu CHN
5th Todd Holzapfel AUS

1993 TAKAPUNA, NEW ZEALAND
1st Thomas Johanson FIN
2nd Peter Tanscheit BRA
3rd Robert Scheidt BRA
4th Nikolas Burfoot NZL
5th Michael Hestbaek DEN

Women
1st Carolijn Brouwer NED
2nd Giselle Camet USA
3rd Alexandra Verbeek NED
4th Maria Vlachou GRE
5th Jacqueline Ellis AUS

Laser Radial
1st Ben Ainslie GBR
2nd Daniel Slater NZL
3rd Allan Coutts NZL
4th Michael Blackburn AUS
5th Peter Waring NZL

1991 PORTO CARRAS, GREECE
1st Peter Tanscheit BRA
2nd Stefan Warkalla GER
3rd Mladen Makjanic CRO
4th Michael Hestbaek DEN
5th Dimitri Theodorakis GRE

Women
1st Maria Vlachou GRE
2nd Carolijn Brouwer NED
3rd Ourania Flabouri GRE
4th Roberta Zucchinetti ITA
5th Marina Psichogiou GRE

Laser Radial
1st Stewart Casey AUS
2nd Maria Vlachou GRE
3rd John Karageorgis GRE
4th Alessandro Sartorelli ITA
5th Elias Katchorhis GRE

1990 NEWPORT, USA
1st Glenn Bourke AUS
2nd Steven Bourdow USA
3rd Peter Tanscheit BRA
4th Mark Brink USA
5th Steve Rich GBR

Women
1st Ardis Bollweg NED
2nd Ulrika Antonsson SWE
3rd Jacqueline Ellis AUS
4th Shona Moss CAN
5th Lotta Nilsson SWE

Laser Radial
1st Peter Katcha USA
2nd John Bonds USA
3rd Scott Cheney USA
4th Ardis Bollweg NED
5th Ulrika Antonsson SWE

WORLD MASTERS
1999 MELBOURNE, AUSTRALIA

Grand Masters
1st Graham Oborn AUS
2nd Jack Hansen NZL
3rd Keith Vann NZL
4th Ben Piefke AUS
5th Kerry Waraker AUS

Masters
1st Keith Wilkins GBR
2nd Peter Sundeim SWE
3rd Doug Peckover USA
4th Jack Schlachter AUS
5th Timothy Alexander AUS

Apprentices
1st Mark Littlejohn GBR
2nd Andreas John GER
3rd Alan Davis GBR
4th Bill O'Hara IRL
5th Brad Taylor AUS

Laser Radial
1st Mark Orams NZL
2nd Alexandre Nikolaev RUS
3rd Frank Inmon AUS
4th Wilmar Groenendijk NED
5th Adam French AUS

Women
1st Lyndall Patterson AUS
2nd Helen Cooksey AUS
3rd Sally Sharp USA
4th Susan Fielding AUS
5th Lesley Hotchin GBR

Great Grand Masters
1st Graham Read AUS
2nd Haruyoshi Kimura JPN
3rd Geoffrey Myburgh RSA
4th Kurt Zueger SUI
5th Peter O'Grady AUS

1997 ALGARROBO, CHILE

Grand Masters
1st Colin Lovelady AUS
2nd Peter Seidenberg USA
3rd Wilhelm Gerlinger GER
4th Joe Van Rossem CAN
5th Jack Hansen NZL

Masters
1st Doug Peckover USA
2nd Mark Bethwaite AUS
3rd Keith Wilkins GBR
4th Jack Schlachter AUS
5th Barry Waller AUS

Apprentices
1st Herman Cristian GER
2nd Alan Davis GBR
3rd Marcelo Fuchs BRA
4th Terry Scutcher GBR
5th Bill O'Hara IRL

Laser Radial
1st Wilmar Groenendjyk NED
2nd Aydin Yurdum TUR
3rd Alexandre Nikolaev RUS
4th Gary McCrohon AUS
5th Heinz Gebauer CAN

1996 CAPE TOWN, SOUTH AFRICA

Grand Masters
1st Ben Piefke AUS
2nd Denis O'Sullivan IRL
3rd Colin Lovelady AUS
4th Peter Seidenberg USA
5th Ken Holiday RSA

Masters
1st Keith Wilkins GBR
2nd Mark Bethwaite AUS
3rd Alan Keen RSA
4th Barry Waller AUS
5th Doug Peckover USA

Apprentices
1st Peter Wilson RSA
2nd Robert Douglass AUS
3rd Regis Berenguier FRA
4th Terry Scutcher GBR
5th Chris Rodowicz AUS

Laser Radial
1st Adam French AUS
2nd Alexandre Nikolaev RUS
3rd Kevin Bloor AUS
4th Rui Sancho ANG
5th Gary McCrohon AUS

1995 TENERIFE, CANARY ISLANDS

Grand Masters
1st Colin Lovelady AUS
2nd Peter Seidenberg USA
3rd Jack Hansen NZL
4th Joe Van Rossem CAN
5th Michael Heath AUS

Masters
1st Keith Wilkins GBR
2nd Barry Waller AUS
3rd Ted Moore USA
4th Pieter Dekker NED
5th Jacky Nebrel FRA

Apprentices
1st Nicholas Harrison GBR
2nd Lance Burger RSA
3rd Tomas Franzen SWE
4th Peter Saxton GBR
5th Norio Akiyama JPN

1994 WAKAYAMA, JAPAN

Grand Masters
1st Colin Lovelady AUS
2nd Peter Seidenberg USA
3rd Dennis O'Sullivan IRL
4th Barry Pownall AUS
5th Tony Denham AUS

Masters
1st Keith Wilkins GBR
2nd Hiroyuki Uehara JPN
3rd Mark Bethwaite AUS
4th Katsumi Hirano JPN
5th Ian Rawet GBR

Apprentices
1st Norio Akiyama JPN
2nd Nicholas Harrison GBR
3rd Nelson Horn Ilha BRA
4th Koichiro Naito JPN
5th Doug Peckover USA

1993 TAKAPUNA, NEW ZEALAND

Great Grand Masters
1st Doug Bates NZL
2nd Robert Saltmarsh USA

Grand Masters
1st Colin Lovelady AUS
2nd Dennis O'Sullivan IRL
3rd Barry Pownall AUS
4th Ralph Ellis AUS
5th John Maynard GBR

Masters
1st Keith Wilkins GBR
2nd John Rigg AUS
3rd Mark Bethwaite AUS
4th Barry Waller AUS
5th John Douglas NZL

Apprentices
1st Paul Page NZL
2nd Neville Wittey AUS
3rd Murray Thom NZL
4th Andrew York AUS
5th Lance Burger USA

Women
1st Jill Robertson CAN
2nd Sally Sharp USA

1991 PORTO CARRAS, GREECE

Grand Masters
1st Colin Lovelady AUS
2nd Friedhelm Lixenfeld GER
3rd Heinz Gebauer CAN
4th Nick Paine GBR
5th Tony Denham AUS

Masters
1st Keith Wilkins GBR
2nd Peter Seidenberg CAN
3rd Barry Waller AUS
4th Willi Gerlinger GER
5th Ilkka Schroderus FIN

Apprentices
1st Stephen Birbeck GBR
2nd Mark Phillips AUS
3rd Mario Orlich ITA
4th Geoffrey McGillivray AUS
5th Peter Wolfe IRL

1990 NEW BEDFORD, MA

Grand Masters
1st Friedhelm Lixenfeld GER
2nd Jim Christopher USA
3rd Tony Denham AUS
4th Norman Freeman USA

5th Nick Paine GBR

Masters
1st Dennis O'Sullivan IRL
2nd Peter Seidenberg CAN
3rd Joe Van Rossem CAN
4th Curt Blidner SWE
5th David Olson USA

Apprentices
1st Kim Zetterberg USA
2nd Michael Stovin-Bradford AUS
3rd Mark Phillips AUS
4th Geoffrey McGillivray AUS
5th Had Brick USA

U.S. NATIONAL CHAMPIONSHIPS

1998 Osterville, MA
1st John Torgerson USA
2nd Andy Lovell USA
3rd Mike Simms USA

1997 Long Beach, CA
1st Alex Camet USA
2nd Paul Zambrski USA
3rd Alax Ascensios USA

1996 Richmond, CA
1st Orlando Gledhill CAN
2nd Steve Bourdow USA
3rd Duncan Pearce CAN

1995 Annapolis, MD
1st Mark Mendelblatt
2nd Andy Lovell
3rd Kevin Hall

1994 Marina del Rey, CA
1st Nick Adamson
2nd Alex Ascencios
3rd Andy Lovell

1993 Nashville, TN
1st Peter Dreyfuss
2nd Alex Ascencios
3rd Mike Uzniz

1992 Toms River, NJ
1st Max Skelley
2nd Bern Noack
3rd Martin Hartmanis

1991 Ft. Walton Beach, FL
1st Andy Lovell
2nd Scott Kyle
3rd Brett Davis

1990 Richmond, CA
1st Mark Brink
2nd Sam Kerner
3rd Rohan Lord

NORTH AMERICAN CHAMPIONSHIPS

1998 VICTORIA, CANADA
1st Bernard Luttmer CAN
2nd Cameron Dunn NZL
3rd Edward Wright GBR
4th Bill Hardesty USA
5th Jason Rhodes CAN

1997 GALVESTON BAY, TX
1st Mike Simms USA
2nd Cameron Dunn NZL
3rd John Torrenson USA
4th John Myrdal USA
5th Allan Coutts NZL

1996 LITTLE EGG, NJ
1st Nick Adamson
2nd Bern Noack
3rd Brett Davis
4th Jamie Boyden
5th Marty Essig

1995 SAN FRANCISCO, CA
1st Kevin Hall
2nd Steve Bourdow
3rd Russ Silvestri
4th Kris Decke
5th Adam Beashel

1994 WESTPORT, CT
1st David Loring
2nd Rod Davies
3rd Mark Mendelblatt
4th Max Skelley
5th Scott Milnes

1993 MANITOBA, CANADA
1st Rod Davies
2nd Ray Davies
3rd Jason Rhodes
4th Eric Naranjo
5th Michael Simms

1992 EUGENE, OR
1st Carl Buchan
2nd Mark Brink
3rd Randy Lake
4th Dave Watt
5th George Szabo

1991 KINGSTON, CANADA
1st Kevin Hall
2nd Andy Lovell
3rd Ray Davies
4th Bern Noack
5th Steve Bourdow

1990 BARRINGTON, RI
1st Sam Kerner
2nd Rohan Lord
3rd Stephen Bourdow
4th Glenn Bourke
5th Rod Davies

EUROPEAN CHAMPIONSHIPS

1998 BREITENBRUNN, AUSTRIA
1st Ben Ainslie GBR
2nd Karl Suneson SWE
3rd Andreas Geritzer AUT
4th Adonis Bougiouris GRE
5th Peer Moberg NOR

1997 CAISCAIS, PORTUGAL
1st Hugh Styles GBR
2nd Stefan Warkall GER
3rd Ben Ainslie GBR
4th Vasco Serpa POR
5th Xavier LeClair FRA

1996 QUIBERON, FRANCE
1st Ben Ainslie GBR
2nd Francesco Bruni ITA
3rd Stefan Warkalla GER
4th Roope Suomalainen FIN
5th Tamas Eszes HUN

Laser Radial
1st Samuel Lelievre FRA
2nd Pasquale Chila ITA
3rd Filipe Silva POR
4th Raimondas Siugzdinis LTU
5th Selim Kakis TUR

Women
1st Cristiana Monina ITA
2nd Larissa Nevierov ITA
3rd Jeanette Dagson SWE
4th Anne Le Helley FRA
5th Tatiana Veselova RUS

1995 ISTANBUL, TURKEY
1st John Harrysson SWE
2nd Klaus Lahme GER
3rd Hugh Styles GBR

4th Karl Suneson SWE
5th Stefan Warkalla GER

Laser Radial
1st Selim Kakis TUR
2nd Kazuyoshi Nakao JPN
3rd Stelios Karakasidis GRE
4th Raimondas Siugzdinis LTU
5th Julien Bicler FRA

Women
1st Larissa Nevierov ITA
2nd Efi Mantzaraki GRE
3rd Deniz Karacaoglu TUR
4th Cristiana Monina ITA
5th Tatiana Vesselova RUS

1994 HAYLING ISLAND, UK
1st Francesco Bruni ITA
2nd Eivind Melleby NOR
3rd Terje Andre Kjaer NOR
4th Serge Kats NED
5th Daniel Birgmark SWE

Laser Radial
1st Gustavo Lima POR
2nd Rodion Luka UKR
3rd Olivier Poullain FRA
4th Benoit Raphalen FRA
5th Pierre Joseph FRA

Women
1st Roberta Hartley GBR
2nd Lucia del Vecchio ITA
3rd Larissa Nevierov ITA
4th Mieke Clark GBR
5th Catherine Grime GBR

1993 CAGLIARI, ITALY
1st John Harrysson SWE
2nd Ghris Gowers GBR
3rd Pascal Lacoste FRA
4th Thomas Johanson FIN
5th Richard Stenhouse GBR

Laser Radial
1st Ben Ainslie GBR
2nd Cyrille Caujolle FRA
3rd Rodion Luka UKR
4th Jean-Philippe Klein FRA
5th Vasiliy Gereluk UKR

Women
1st Larissa Nevierov ITA
2nd Penny Mountford GBR
3rd Larissa Moscalenko RUS
4th Maria Vlachou GRE
5th Catherine Grime GBR

1992 MARIESTAD, SWEDEN
1st Thomas Johanson FIN
2nd Stefan Warkalla GER
3rd Michael Hestbaek DEN
4th Nikolas Burfoot GBR
5th John Harrysson SWE

Laser Radial
1st Carolijn Brouwer NED
2nd Ben Ainslie GBR
3rd Giuseppe Manzo ITA
4th Thierry Peyre FRA
5th Mattia Carpini ITA

Women
1st Carolijn Brouwer NED
2nd Roberta Zucchinetti ITA
3rd Ardis Bollweg NED
4th Alexandra Verbeek NED
5th Maria Vlachou GRE

1991 EL MASNOU, SPAIN
1st Thomas Johanson FIN
2nd Simon Bowes-Cole GBR
3rd Nikos Nikoltsoudis GRE
4th Stefan Warkalla GER
5th Pascal Lacoste FRA

Laser Radial
Workum, Holland
1st Dimitrios Theodorakis GRE
2nd Frank Lefebvre FRA
3rd Freek de Miranda NED
4th Michel Vatinel FRA
5th Mattia Carpini ITA

Women
1st Roberta Zucchinetti ITA
2nd Nicolette Deliyanni GRE
3rd Ardis Bollweg NED
4th Alexandra Verbeek NED
5th Marie Dahllof SWE

1990 LORIENT, FRANCE
1st Tim Powell GBR
2nd Michael Hestbaek DEN
3rd Mike Budd GBR
4th Mladen Makjanic YUG
5th Stefan Warkalla GER

Laser Radial
1st Rikkert Graat NED
2nd Giannia Karageorgis GRE
3rd Jort Scharffordt NED
4th Franck Lefebre FRA
5th Stefane Francois FRA

Women
1st Lotta Nilsson SWE

2nd Larissa Nevierov ITA
3rd Luisa Spanghero ITA
4th Marie Dahllof SWE
5th Pascale Dentraygues FRA

EUROPEAN YOUTH CHAMPIONSHIPS
1998 BREITENBRUNN, AUSTRIA
1st Joonas Paivarinta FIN
2nd Matt Howard GBR
3rd Gareth Blanckenberg RSA
4th Daniel Holman GBR
5th Felix Pruvot FRA

1997 CAISCAIS, PORTUGAL
1st Peter Walker GBR
2nd Nicolas Dumonceau BEL
3rd Joonas Paivarinta FIN
4th Lazaros Charalambidis GRE
5th Vagelis Chimonas GRE

1996 HIGHCLIFFE, UK

Standard Rig
1st Alexandros Logothetis GRE
2nd Rasmus Myrgren SWE
3rd Brad Funk USA
4th Owen Modral GBR
5th Pavel Lazarski POL

Radial Rig
1st Marc de Haas NED
2nd Beniot Raphalen FRA
3rd Justin Deal GBR
4th Nicolas Pennec FRA
5th Salvatore D'Amico ITA

1995 VARBERG, SWEDEN

Standard Rig
1st Andrew Geritzer AUT
2nd Alexandros Logothetis GRE
3rd Christian Wetzel GER
4th Magnus Nilsson SWE
5th Paul Goodison GBR

Radial Rig
1st Pierre Joseph FRA
2nd Beniot Raphalen FRA
3rd Stelios Karakasidis GRE
4th Mathias Stepanek AUT
5th Guillaume Chiellino FRA

1994 WORKUM, HOLLAND

Standard Rig
1st Philipp Buchert GER

2nd Jan-Willem Harwijne NED
3rd Tamas Eszes HUN
4th Ori Gal ISR
5th Rui Coelho POR

Radial Rig
1st Samuel Lelievre FRA
2nd Pierre Joseph FRA
3rd Gustovo Roxo de Lima POR
4th Pierre-Laurent Garnero FRA
5th Herve Piveteau FRA

1993 NEUSIEDLER SEE, AUSTRIA

Standard Rig
1st Karl Suneson SWE
2nd Neil Coxon GBR
3rd Alistair Coates GBR
4th Daniel Bjoerndahl SWE
5th Mark Barron GBR

Radial Rig
1st Ben Ainslie GBR
2nd Henrique Anjos POR
3rd Jean-Philippe Michel FRA
4th Pierre Joseph FRA
5th Pierre-Laurent Garnero FRA

1992 MOSS, NORWAY

Standard Rig
1st Karl Suneson SWE
2nd Hugh Styles GBR
3rd Neil Coxon GBR
4th Johan Weimann DEN
5th Pieter Lantermans NED

Radial Rig
1st Roberta Zucchinetti ITA
2nd Antonis Logothetis GRE
3rd Ben Ainslie GBR
4th Alistair Coates GBR
5th Andrew Simpson GBR

1991 NIEUWPOORT, BELGIUM
1st I. Karageorgis. GRE
2nd K. Suneson SWE
3rd A. Bougiouris GRE
4th T. Van de Voorde BEL
5th O. Papadopoulos GRE

1990 IZMIR, TURKEY
1st Emilios Papathanassiou GRE
2nd Gareth Greenfield GBR
3rd Craig Mitchell GBR
4th Andrew Oddie GBR
5th Giancarlo Simeoli ITA

CANADIAN NATIONAL CHAMPIONSHIPS

1998 Manitoba
1st Bill Hardesty USA
2nd Mike Simms CAN
3rd Chris Cook CAN

1997 Ontario
1st Michael Simms
2nd Tommy Wharton
3rd Ray Davies

1996 Nova Scotia
1st Nick Pullen
2nd Jamie Boyden
3rd Mike Simms

1995 Victoria
1st Rod Dawson
2nd Jason Rhodes
3rd Steve Bourdow

1994 Toronto
1st Rod Davies
2nd Peter Hurley
3rd Mike Kalin

1993 Kingston
1st Max Skelley
2nd Rod Davies
3rd Steve Bourdow

1992 Lunenburg
1st Ray Davies
2nd Orlando Gledhill
3rd Max Skelley

1991 Beaconsfield
1st Nick Adamson
2nd Philip Karcher
3rd Nicolas Pullen

1990 Kingston
1st Rod Davies
2nd Scott Ellis
3rd Brad Kitchen

APPENDIX 2

International Laser Class Association

The International Laser Class Association (ILCA) is a worldwide club of Laser owners. They work voluntarily, organizing races, training, putting out newsletters, and ensuring that the Laser remains in demand and is strictly controlled by class rules so your investment in the boat is protected.

The ILCA goals are: to enhance the enjoyment of Laser sailboats; to provide a means of exchanging information among Laser sailors around the world; to promote and encourage Laser class racing in all countries under uniform rules; and to promote and encourage the sporting and recreational aspects of sailing.

The contact for the International Laser Class Association is

Jeff Martin
ILCA
P.O. Box 26
Falmouth, Cornwall TR11 3TN
England

44 (0)1326 315064 (phone)
44 (0) 1326 318968 (fax)
E-mail: ilca@easynet.co.uk
http://www.laserinternational.org

National and regional associations exist for the same purpose. National associations have their own newsletters, fixture lists, and information of all kinds for Laser owners. Addresses for these can be found at the ILCA website or by contacting the International Class office directly.

The contact for the North American region is

Fred Schroth
5205 Beacon Drive
Austin, TX 78734
512-266-8254 (phone and fax)
E-mail: laserclass@laser.org
http://www.laser.org
home page: http://laser@laser.org/

I would encourage anyone who sails a Laser or Laser Radial to join your national association. Membership in the North American Region includes membership in the International Laser Class Association.

Index